A LOVE LIKE THIS

BY: Jennifer Willis

A LOVE LIKE THIS

Cover by: Jennifer Willis

Edited by: Jennifer Willis

Photos owned by: Jennifer Willis

Art By: Jennifer Willis

ISBN: 979-8-9891923-0-4

LIBRARY OF CONGRESS 202391718

🦋 *TABLE OF CONTENTS* 🦋 *A LOVE LIKE THIS* 🦋

IN A WORLD WHERE THERE IS PAIN, YOU COMFORTED

IN A WORLD WHERE I FELT LOST, YOU FOUND ME

IN A WORLD WHERE THERE WAS DOUBT, YOU BELIEVED

IN A WORLD WHERE THERE IS KINDNESS, YOU SPREAD IT

IN A WORLD WHERE THERE WAS HATRED, YOU LOVED

IN A WORLD WHERE THERE IS END, YOU SHOWED ME ETERNITY

A devoted daughter's journey through intense grief to finding that love has no end. Come along as she fights to save her Mother and learns that she never has to say goodbye.

I LOVE YOU ENDLESSLY

CHAPTER 1
An Angel

In July of 1932, a beautiful blonde-haired, green-eyed baby girl was born in a colonial home overlooking the beautiful harbor in Newport, Rhode Island. It was a hot day when pure wonder entered this world. I believe that was the day Jesus sent an angel to act out a plan, for this wasn't just any baby. This baby was special, a true gift from God. Victoria would grace us with her earthly presence for eighty-five years. Victoria was named after her Father's Mother, whom he adored. She was a happy, sweet baby with large green eyes, a beautiful cherub-like face framed with perfect blonde curls, and a smile that would light up a room. Her Mother, Theresa, would often remark, "This baby is so different from my other children. She's so pleasant and content." In the 1930s, in a sleepy, waterfront, historic town, one could put their baby outside in the carriage on a warm, sunny day. Victoria would lay smiling sweetly, contently, looking up at the clear blue sky as the warm sun shone down on her tiny cheeks. "She hardly cries," her mother would say, a complete joy. Theresa and Cyril found themselves in love with this new little angel.

Victoria was the third girl of four, which meant Victoria's Mother was a busy lady. Her first baby was a little boy, who she lost as he passed in her arms, of unknown cause. Theresa would always miss her firstborn, but having the girls was a blessing. They would be dressed alike on Sunday as they all walked along Bellevue Avenue, in their best on their way to worship the Lord. From the young age of two, Victoria loved to sing. She'd sing along or hum if she didn't know the words, and although just a toddler, she sang on tune. Victoria would love to sing while skipping down the cobblestone streets. She did this daily, not thinking anyone had noticed, as she was just a little girl enjoying the pureness of childhood. One day, while skipping and singing, a neighbor called out to Victoria, "Well, there she is, the little songbird." Victoria was shocked and embarrassed. She ran home to tell her Mother about the man up the street who had heard her singing. Victoria's Mother laughed and assured her that the man must have enjoyed listening to her sing. Victoria would soon promise to always be watchful as to who could hear her sweet voice.

That watchfulness comes to an end as she moves into her teenage years. Victoria decides to take piano lessons and finds another talent. Victoria would fill her home with beautiful music, having excelled in her new skill. She would sit on her piano bench, singing like a bird, while she elegantly played the keys. Her older sister, Irma, sometimes joined in, as did her Father. Her Mom, Theresa, sings along but is best known for humming. Many happy days were enjoyed in the parlor as a family, but if you were ever looking for Victoria, you'd know where to find her, just listen for the songbird. Victoria is now in high school and quite an accomplished pianist with the voice of an opera singer. Catholic school was not an easy way to be educated. The nuns were strict, and Victoria was a sensitive young lady but obedient nonetheless. During choir, the nuns quickly zoned in on Victoria's voice. Eyebrows lifting, the sisters all agreed that Victoria was the one they would use for their solo performances. To Victoria's dismay, the nuns, or sisters, as addressed, demanded a lot once they found strength in one of their students. Victoria would soon find herself on stage, singing, playing the piano, and taking the lead in the operettas. The town folks clapped loudly, as did her family. The sisters smiled, and Victoria obediently walked offstage. Victory felt good, but it never called Victoria's name. Solo performances were not her forte as her nerves were always present, but she'd push through. Victoria rarely started anything she couldn't finish. So she forged on knowing what was expected of her, delivering beautifully, although apprehensive.

Victoria taught herself how to sew. She would sit for hours making doll clothes as a younger girl, and now that she was a teenager, she could sew beautiful gifts for her family. Victoria had three sisters, and they would ask her to hem their dresses or alter them to fit. She made her own skirts and clothing for her family. The clothes were all beautifully sewn and so very appreciated. She also taught herself to knit, and this found her creating beautiful sweaters, afghans, and more. Victoria loved being creative, and it showed in everything she achieved. She was happy and confident yet shy and reserved. A lovely girl, she made her parents proud.

CHAPTER 2

Young Love

She was sixteen and beautiful. Her curly blonde hair was now shoulder length, and those green eyes were just a forest of beauty. A faithful and religious young lady, indeed. Victoria had high morals, and she wasn't about to change. Fun was never out of the question. Her friends and she would go to the local café to get a fountain drink and ice cream and would head over to the local Catholic Academy for boys to watch the basketball games or attend local dances. One evening, Victoria and her friends were chatting at the local dance. Victoria noticed two very handsome boys smiling at her. She knew the name of one young man but not the other. He approached her, and she thought quickly, feeling a bit anxious. One of the boys walked over to Victoria, and she nervously asked, "You are Richie, aren't you?" But to her surprise, he answered, "No, I'm Bill." After their awkward introduction, they danced a few dances, and smiling, they parted ways for the evening.

It wasn't long before the couple became inseparable, and a courtship ensued. Victoria attended the basketball games, cheering Bill on, as he was one of the top players at De LaSalle Academy. Love was definitely in the air. Evenings and weekends were enjoyable, walking through Newport's cobblestone streets, getting Chinese chow mein sandwiches, and being kissed on the cheek on her front porch before parting. Graduating from High School with honors, they were both straight-A students. Bill knew from the day he laid eyes on Victoria, that she was the one. The same night they met, he said to his friend, "See that girl over there? That's the girl I'm going to marry." Bill let her know all the time that she was special, so before the Navy called Bill to service, he made sure to ask Victoria if she would be his forever. Victoria gladly accepted and with the ring on her finger, tried to imagine what the future held for them. Bill starts his four-year journey with the Navy.

While Bill was away, Victoria worked for the telephone company as a switchboard operator and later a lumber company and a bank. She loved her work and excelled at both, but couldn't wait to see her beloved Bill. She'd listened to music, such as "He's Just My Bill," and many others they danced to. Victoria had a wedding to plan, which kept her busy and gave her something to look forward to. While daily life goes on, many letters are exchanged, and the picture above Bill's bunk keeps his focus on the girl back home, soon to be his wife. Bill is allowed some leave and comes home to help with the wedding plans. St. Mary's is a beautiful, historic church. This large church, made of stone, was the church Victoria attended while growing up and was the obvious choice for their wedding day. Bill was of the Protestant faith. He decided that he desired to share the same beliefs to raise their family, so he took classes in Catholicism and soon was baptized Catholic. Sharing faith felt like a great foundation, to start the young couple on their new life together. Soon, the couple finds themselves trying to establish a date for the big day. They visited their local priest and requested a day in September 1953.

The priest told them that "an admired" couple was looking at that date, but since they were local and a part of the congregation, they would get first choice. Bill and Victoria happily accepted. Bill and Victoria are surprised to learn that the "admired" couple were Jacqueline Bouvier and John F. Kennedy. Victoria and Bill had their little claim to fame, and the story was one they loved to tell for many years to come.

CHAPTER 3

Starting Life Together

On a beautiful, warm September day, in 1953, Bill and Victoria married in St. Mary's Church in Newport, Rhode Island. It was a beautiful wedding, followed by a reception in the garden. This marriage would be the start of a lifelong love.

The newlyweds decided on a trip to New York City for their honeymoon. In my Father's words, here he describes their honeymoon. "During our honeymoon, we stayed at the Hotel New Yorker. When we arrived, we toured Times Square, 34th St, Fifth Avenue, and enjoyed a bit of window shopping. While in Cannes, France, on the Riviera, I met a gentleman who ran a dress company in New York on Broadway. We chatted about our upcoming wedding and the fact that I was from the United States and that we were going to visit New York City on our honeymoon.

He gave me his phone number and told me when we got to New York to be sure to give him a call on the evening of our arrival. When we arrived in New York City, we called our new friend. We decided where to meet, and I was happy to introduce my new wife, Victoria. I remember that he complimented Victoria on her fancy hat and attire, as she was quite fashionable. He made arrangements to get tickets for us. We were thrilled and surprised to receive tickets to two Broadway shows, South Pacific and Picnic. He took us to dinner at an exquisite restaurant, and we were more than impressed. We asked him to order for us, and he gladly obliged. The first thing that came out to us was a glass of tomato juice in a large, silver bowl filled with ice. What a show! The main meal was delicious. We had a lovely dinner and enjoyed each other's company. We expressed our gratitude, and after a lovely evening, we parted ways. Everything was tremendous!

We continued to window shop and went to Macy's and other big stores. We ate at steak houses and other small eateries. We walked through Grand Central Station and looked around. I showed her Madison

Square Garden, where I played basketball in 1950. We played the preliminary round for the Boston Celtics game.

It was the day we beat St. Augustine's in overtime. I was fouled, and the score was tied. I hit the first foul shot to tie the game and hit the second one with a few seconds left. Sixteen thousand people stood and applauded, and we celebrated a huge win. I couldn't wait to show Victoria and share this wonderful memory of mine with my new wife." Upon arriving home from their happy honeymoon, Bill and Victoria watched as the Kennedys married at St. Mary's Church one week after their wedding. A plaque adorns the church today, marking the date of the Kennedy wedding. We always joked with Mom and Dad that they should get a plaque, too.

Shortly after getting married, the newlywed couple was stationed in Florida, at the Green Cove Springs base. Living away would be very different for Victoria, especially in a tiny Quonset hut in hot weather, but they were happy to make it their home. Victoria made curtains for the windows, and soon the cozy place felt like home, well, almost. In Florida, there were "guests" that folks from up North were not used to hosting. Victoria would yell out loud when she was met face-to-face with lizards and water bugs. The locals said water bugs were harmless, just looking for water. Victoria begged to differ, saying, "They gave her the willies."

 Bill made a garden that adorned the outskirts of the Silver Quonset hut and trimmed it with large white stones. Victoria hung laundry out to dry in the hot sun, always keeping an eye out for any new "guests."
Not long after arriving, friendships were established, and Victoria was asked to play the piano and sing church hymns for a local group of folks, trying to better themselves. It wasn't something she was sure of, but they loved her, and soon, she felt herself smiling as she sang worship songs to God and led the group along. It wasn't long before the couple found themselves longing for home. During the evenings, Dad had duty on the ship, and Victoria was frightened in the sparsely populated base. It was dark, and every shadow and

sound was terrifying for a small-town girl who'd never lived alone. Bill would switch duty with other sailors, as much as he could, to make sure those scary nights were few and far between, but he hoped he could ask for a transfer as soon as possible. They spent the rest of the year making the best of it and making memories never forgotten. It wasn't long before the opportunity of a transfer was upon them.

Bill had two choices, and neither was guaranteed. Newport was one of them. Keeping their fingers crossed, they waited. Mom was so hopeful and kept her Mother updated daily. They held their breath until the day Bill came home with an exciting surprise. He got Newport as a transfer! They were going home.

They packed up, said goodbye, and boarded the train for the long but happy ride home. Upon arriving home and finding an apartment, they settled in and breathed a sigh of relief. Now safely back in Newport, they would no longer experience hot days in the metal Quonset hut. Mom was relieved not to be alone at night, and bugs up North were more tolerable. They were thrilled to be with family, familiar faces and places, with new memories to make. While Bill was in the Navy traveling, the home base was a welcomed move. Victoria continued to work, all while missing her new husband but spending quality time with family, and for this, she was grateful.

A memory that always made Mom smile was when her Mother wanted new furniture a friend was selling from an estate. It was beautiful but wasn't a necessity. Theresa decided that purchasing the parlor set would have to wait, but Victoria surprised her Mother and bought it for her. Theresa was delighted, as Mom put it, and Mom was thrilled to be able to spoil her Mother, with her own hard-earned money. Married life finds them happy, and after three years, Victoria finds she is carrying their first child. In July of 1957, their first daughter, Julie, was born. Looking just like her Daddy, they couldn't be happier, and life with their first baby gets underway. Victoria and Theresa take many walks that summer with Julie in the carriage under the warm summer sun. Soon, Fall arrives, and they are all looking forward to the baby's first Christmas.

Mom finds herself with an uneasy feeling these days and can't quite put her finger on it. It's a feeling of heaviness she feels she is carrying, and she voices her concerns to her Mother. Her Mother assures her it's a new Mother's heart, just worry that comes along with having a new baby, and that it's completely normal. Victoria knew it wasn't that, but what was it?

On a chilly November day, Victoria is up early, bathing her now almost four-month-old baby. Victoria thought about calling her Mother, but they were expecting her shortly, and Bill suggested she hold off, as she would be arriving soon. Theresa was home playing solitaire, waiting for her husband and daughter, who had gone out on that crisp autumn morning.

Theresa always knocks with the same knock, so you always knew it was her. Bum, but a bum bum, bum bum. Mom calls out to Dad, "Bill, someone's at the door. It must be my Mother and Daddy." Bill checks the door to find no one there, but since they live in an apartment, they assume they have heard a neighbor's visitor. They go about their routine when this time, Mom hears that signature knock. Bum, but a bum bum, bum bum.

"For heaven's sake, Bill, answer the door. My Mother's here." Bill checked the door again, but there was no one there. Soon again, a knock, but a different one, and Bill checks. He opens the door to find the priest, Victoria's Dad, and sister, delivering the news that Theresa, Mom's dear Mother, is gone. While playing solitaire, Theresa called the ambulance as she wasn't feeling well. Shortly after arriving at the hospital, an embolism took her life, and the day she had planned, was suddenly stolen from them all.

Mom screams in disbelief, and the next few days are filled with tears, sleepless nights, and questions. Why hadn't she called? She was supposed to be coming over! We had plans! Although the days were the saddest she'd ever known, and her heart was beyond shattered, her newborn baby kept her spirits in check. She still had to get out of bed, to tend to the baby, and just the sight of her made her smile. One day, after going through that terrible day in her head over and over, the memory of that day reminded her of those familiar knocks on the door.

Could it be? No, the common sense side of her intervenes. No, it had to be the neighbor's visitor.

But wait, the familiar knock, no one there? Minutes later, the priest arrives at the door with the terrible news. Could it be? Was Theresa coming by to say goodbye? No, it had to be the neighbors. But the neighbors soon confirmed they had no visitors. It was the familiar knock, and she was saying goodbye. Victoria soon realizes that the uneasy feeling she was carrying is no longer there. It was gone. That uncomfortable feeling she had felt for months had left when her Mother passed away.

The love between a Mother and child is like no other, and the heart feels the strain when the cord is fragile. The heart knows when the invisible cord is stretching too far and cries out to keep it near. When the very heartbeat that surrounds you from the beginning of time starts to fade, a part of us also fades. The two heartbeats have always been in sync, always dependent on each other. An experience that transcends over the years, an invisible connection that distance nor time will ever break. No matter how stretched, it remains....unbroken.

Sometimes, the pain of suddenly losing her Mom at the very young age of fifty-two hurt more than she could've ever imagined. Passing folks soon caught her eye. Was that her? Her heart would skip a beat as she realized it wasn't and never would be. Picking up the phone to tell Mom what fun things the baby did often led to tears when she remembered her Mom wasn't there, and life became very different. A new wife, a new Mother, and undying faith get her through, and day by day, Victoria moves forward.

CHAPTER 4

Babies

As Julie turned three, Mom was happy to find she was carrying her second child. The birth of their son was a quick one. Dad went to sign Mom in, and when he returned minutes later, the nurse was walking towards him. "Congratulations, you have a son!" Dad was surprised and rushed to be with Victoria and their new son. They named him Kenneth, and he was "as blonde as the sun," as Mom would say, with long brown eyes, and favored Victoria. A beautiful baby, Kenny had many allergies, and sleepless nights made for exhaustion. Soon, the allergies were addressed and remedied. Kenny would turn into a rambunctious, happy little guy, doing wild things boys do. Mom would often wake to the sound of two-year-old Kenny riding his rocking horse like a wild little cowboy at 3:00 a.m. She would smile sleepily and get him settled back into his crib, only to wake to a new day full of surprises from her active toddler.

During the day Victoria kept busy with her little ones. Singing lullabies and dancing with her babies is what she lived for. Her faith was always so strong. She often thought she would join the convent, but the thought of not having children wasn't anything she wanted to imagine. Her babies gave her immense joy, and she loved them with all her heart.

During the summer, Bill worked for a moving company while he attended college on an athletic scholarship. Nights were busy, and Victoria would sit at the kitchen table and help Bill study for his tests. They would go over foreign languages together, and she would quiz him for hours. They were in this together, and she supported his education entirely. When Dad received his degree, Mom received a certificate recognizing her role in helping her husband through college. They were so proud and felt they had achieved this impressive milestone as a team. Mom always said, some of the best things they did, they did together. Victoria and Bill often took walks in the evening with the children before the sunset. Hand in hand, they would walk to a neighborhood one street over from their apartment, where new homes were being constructed.

One house, in particular, was for sale, and well, you guessed it, they bought it. 1961 was the year, and the young couple with two children were living their best life.

A white Cape Cod home with black shutters was to be their home together for over 60 years. Dad painted the house a beautiful yellow, with white shutters. A white, iron railing framed the brick steps and dressed up the entrance. A white picket fence surrounded the backyard, and trees were planted with beautiful gardens. A clothesline and swing set followed. A beagle mix soon joined the family, and they named her Penny, as she was copper colored. The children loved Penny, and she grew up right alongside them. Life was feeling great and moving right along.

In September 1965, Victoria took a spill on the stairs and broke her leg. Soon after the fall, she discovered she was carrying their third child. Yes, you guessed it, me. They were thrilled to be adding another baby, and at thirty-three years old, the clock was ticking. This pregnancy was difficult. A broken leg with a large cast, with constant nausea and vomiting, made life complicated.

Eating well wasn't easy because Mom couldn't keep anything down, except steak and puffed rice cereal, for the entire pregnancy. One day, in particular, Victoria was ill. Bill opened the bathroom door, and his heart broke for his wife."You poor thing, it can't be much longer." Days later, they induced her, and, at full term, her third baby was born.

With a head full of dark hair and a round face, folks at the hospital commented on the little Asian baby through the nursery window. Mom would laugh and say, "She's mine." Mom was blonde-haired and would chuckle, "They must think I'm married to an Asian man." It wasn't until Dad was there one day that it all made sense. The same admirers approached Mom, "Oh, now we see who the baby looks like." Dad had a head full of black hair, and I was the image of him.

Back in her room, Mom was looking for a menu. She couldn't wait to eat! Pen in hand, she checked off all she could, and the nurses laughed, "You're gonna eat all that?" They'd exclaim. "You bet! After nine months of steak and puffed rice cereal, I can't wait!" With new energy, Victoria was thrilled, and they brought home their new baby girl, Jennifer, to complete their family.

The kids loved her. Julie was nine, Kenny was four, and he was smitten. Mom said Ken loved me and would often try to pick me up. One day, Mom found Kenny gently caressing my face. She didn't want to startle him, so she whispered, "Isn't she cute, Ken?" he replied, "She's so tender, Mom, so tender." Mom loved that moment and often told the story. A memory dear to her heart. I was a happy baby, and life was moving quickly for this young family.

Shortly after I turned one, Mom's Father, whom we called Gramp, had a terrible stroke. The stroke left him unable to use one side of his body. He was young, and it hit hard. Gramps, the once active man who loved to walk and play with his grandchildren, was now dependent on others. Gramp lived with us for years. My beautiful room, decorated for a princess, was soon changed into a room for Gramp. A large hospital bed and healthcare equipment filled the room. We loved Gramp and loved having him live with us. It was a lot of work for Mom, caring for three children, a household, and a sick Father. Mom and Dad had their work cut out, but Gramps was appreciative. After dinner, Dad would often help bathe Gramp, getting him ready for the evening. The help allowed Mom time with her children.

With the day behind them, Mom could finally rest, and this would find us playing chess with Gramp. He was good at it, taught us, and we all enjoyed it. Gramps was also a great storyteller, and we gathered to listen. He liked to go fishing. Mom and Dad would get him into the car and load the wheelchair into the back of the wagon. Dad wheeled him to the pier while we skipped along. Gramps would happily fish, overlooking the Newport harbor. I imagine it was tremendous work to get him there, but it was so worth it for all of us. We have never forgotten it. Sometimes, the most challenging days are the most memorable days.

CHAPTER 5

Unexpected Illness and Faith

In 1975, Mom started to feel unwell. After all, taking care of three children, a husband, an elderly incapacitated father, and the household, one is bound to get overly tired and more likely to get the flu. Terrible headaches, weakness, and fatigue find Mom at the doctor to try to see what could be going on. Countless tests later, the medical team discovered that she had contracted a rare virus that had affected her spinal cord and heart. Hospitalized, Victoria can't walk and is examined by many specialists. The virus must run its course, but it has done its damage. While hospitalized, I was only nine and traumatized by her absence. Years ago, children could only visit from afar, so when I saw her in a wheelchair, I cried and cried, as did she. We were all frightened of the unknown and wanted her back home with us.

My Grandfather had to go to my Aunt's for care as Mom was fighting to recover. Mom came home weeks later and was still unable to walk. Dad carried her to the bathroom, and when I tickled her feet, she couldn't feel them. I cried every time. Mom needed a lot of rest to recover until her neurological system finally started to respond, and she slowly started to walk again. The virus left her with leg spasms, fatigue, and weakness in the arms and legs. She was different physically and felt it, but true to herself, she fought hard and rallied back. She worked her way up to daily walks, and remarkably, Mom started to feel more like herself. We all had to help with household chores as recovery took time. It would be many years until the virus's long-term effects reared its ugly face.

Returning to normal wasn't easy, but we were a family and moving forward. Where Mom got her strength, we didn't know, but she did. She relied on her faith. Mom always told me she would give it all to God. She would ask for his help and grace to accept what she couldn't change.

She always believed God had a plan and that he was in control. It was never our place to question God's plan. No matter how hard it seems, you must always trust God's decision, as he knows best.

She preached it, but she truly believed it with every fiber of her being, and believe me, NO one could ever convince her of anything different. Her faith never wavered, ever! Even in Mom's darkest times, she knew God had her back. She lived every day, knowing she was loved, and striving to be worthy of a place in his kingdom someday.

Mom decided that she would like to teach religious instruction classes, as she called them. We went every Wednesday after dinner for years to receive education on the Bible. Mom decided she wanted to be a teacher of God's word. She did teach, and she loved it. She was proud to have been able to do something she loved. Teaching the children about God was a wonderful experience. Mom's religious faith was strong, as was her love of the Blessed Mother, to whom she always gave thanks. She would often pray in difficult times to Jesus and the Blessed Mother. When we would ask if her prayers had been answered, Mom always replied, "Thy will be done," and "The good Lord's time is not our time."

She often wore little gold angel pins as a sign of her faith. People would naturally stop and chat with Mom. She was very approachable with her sweet smile, happy voice, and beautiful face. Mom would always take the time to chat with anyone, and if they complimented her on the angel pin, she'd promptly take it off her lapel and give it to that person. Naturally, they would be shocked and insist she keep it, but she'd assure them she had more. If they needed it or wanted it, well then, she wanted them to have it. She was doing the good Lord's work, and she loved it. She'd be so excited to give away those angel pins. Growing up, Mom continued to be a Mother like no other. She would walk up to school holding hands with the neighborhood children surrounding her, as she sang, "Oh, what a beautiful morning, Oh what a beautiful day, I've got a beautiful feeling, everything's going my way!" like a scene straight out of the Sound of Music. This gem of a lady was something unusual. She was my Mother, and I was proud.

When school was out, we arrived home to warm chocolate chip cookies, the sweet aroma filling the air "A nice glass of fresh milk," as she put it, was always close by, and a straw made for a fun time as we made milk bubbles rise out of our cups over the top.

We giggled away, Mom laughing and singing, while we consumed our treat. Mom was always singing, a flowered apron tied around her waist in a bow. She always smelled amazing, like warm, sweet vanilla with a touch of floral.

CHAPTER 6

Baking and Singing

Bread pudding, chocolate-covered brownies, Christmas cookies, all different kinds. Cinnamon sticks and snowballs, lace cookies and sugar, hours and hours, until they came out just right. I remember pans and pans filled with every kind of Christmas cookie you could imagine. The sweet aroma of cinnamon filled the kitchen. With the cookies cooling on the rack, Mom would start with another recipe. We sat by watching all the cookies coming out of the oven, waiting patiently, for Mom to say we could have one. There were many varieties, and this made choosing difficult. We would get to lick the beaters or scrape the bowl in between batches. Dad would come out to the kitchen and pick a favorite, pour a glass of milk, and clear the kitchen, leaving Mom to her masterpieces. When Mom finished making all the delicate, decorative cookies, it would be time to make the fun cookies. Mom would get out all the cookie cutters, and we would press the Santa shape into the soft dough. Next, we would choose a stocking or snowflake.

When the pan was full, the fun-shaped cookies
would go into the oven as we waited excitedly for the
results. When the cookies cooled, we iced them and
decorated them. Cleaning the sprinkles and dried icing
off the table, filling cookie tins, and washing dishes
made for a late evening. Mom would fall into her easy
chair, exhausted, with a feeling of accomplishment. We
always enjoyed watching Mom and participating in the
tradition. When Julie was little, she would pull up a
chair to help Mommy bake. She also loved to help
Mommy with the dishes. A sweet picture holds this
memory like something out of a Norman Rockwell
painting, a beautiful moment. Kenny once tipped over
the baking cabinet as a toddler, only to be covered in
flour and tea bags. Once again, Mom didn't get upset or
scold him instead, she roared in laughter at the image.
She was so tickled to think he looked just like Minnie
Pearl, with that T-bag hanging off his little head.
Shocked and frightened, Mom tended to her little boy.
She was still laughing while she hugged him, assuring
him he was okay while wiping the flour from his face.
Reaching for the broom with a smile," This was one for
the memory book," she would say.

One day, while baking with me as a toddler, Mom had the mixer on the counter with the ingredients for chocolate chip cookies in the bowl. Mom needed to retrieve the vanilla from the cabinet, just a few feet from where I stood on a chair at the counter. Mom gently reminded me not to touch the mixer as she turned her back to open the cabinet. Just then, Mom heard the mixer start. She turned quickly and found me covered in cookie dough and flour. It was in my hair, on my face, on the walls, and on the ceiling. Once again, Mom laughed and got busy cleaning me up and spending the next hour wiping cookie dough off the floor, ceiling, and walls, as she was thinking, This is another memory for that book. Dad came home at three after a day of teaching high school History. He would correct papers, and we could enter the grades into the grade books. I loved doing that. Mom would make dinner some evenings and Dad on others. Prayers first, then we could eat. We talked about our day. Our meals were always homemade, and every Wednesday was spaghetti and meatballs, and Sunday roast and potatoes. The other evenings were fish and vegetables, grilled cheese and soup, sloppy joe sandwiches, pizza, and American chop suey, to name a few.

These were the good old days when families sat down to dinner while chatting about our day. Baths and pj's followed, then Little House on the Prairie, The Waltons, and The Wide World of Disney. When the children were snug in bed, Mom and Dad would watch The Lawrence Welk Show. I would lay in bed listening as they sang songs they knew and loved.

Mom sang all the time, especially in the morning. Her beautiful voice bounding through the house comforted us, whether she knew it or not. The days started early during the school week, and Mom would struggle to get us to wake up as we got older. She'd call upstairs to us, and we'd rise to the smell of breakfast cooking.

We would come downstairs, and there would be Mom, singing along loudly to the old radio, playing John Denver. Apron tied around her waist, spatula in her hand, waiting to flip over chocolate chip, happy-faced pancakes. As we sat at the table with gloomy faces, Mom would deliver the now sad-faced pancakes the warm skillet had created. They always forced a smile and a giggle from us, much to Mom's delight. I hated leaving Mom to go to school.

Most mornings, she would come into my bedroom with my pink canopy bed, matching dresser, and pink and white checkered curtains that she made to dress my windows. She'd pull up the window shades and sing, "Good morning Mary sunshine, it's a beautiful day," and then jump into bed with me, calling me her snuggle bunny. I would beg her to stay home, and she would assure me that school was better than chores. Oh, how I loved being her snuggle bunny! Dad graduated with his Master's in education, and time waited for no one.

CHAPTER 7

Our Very Happy Childhood

We grew up in the sixties and seventies. These had to have been some of the best years for children and families. Our days were pure, and folks were good, simple, and kind. Television programs depicted perfect family lives, and children respected their elders. Summer evenings, we would play outside until the street lights came on, only to hear Mom calling our names throughout the neighborhood. Dinner was waiting, and we came running. Mom and Dad would often put the sprinkler out on summer days. We would spend hours running through the water, spraying about in rotation. The sprinklers in the seventies were metal and had rough metal pieces that sprayed water out while rotating. Penny, our dog, would run over to the spraying water and put her mouth up against the middle part, where the water pressure was the greatest, so she could get a cool drink and bite at this strange contraption that had the children playing excitedly. On the 4th of July, Mom and Dad would get sparklers and light them for us while we ran about the backyard in sheer delight, squealing and making big swirls of sparkly, silver flashes in the night sky. Oh, how we loved those, all while yelling, "Happy 4th of July!" Let me tell you, those days were like no other.

The year following Mom's illness had left me extremely sensitive, and I worried terribly about my Mother. Going to school in the seventies meant sometimes you could walk to school by yourself. On the days when I walked to school by myself, I would get to a location around the corner where I could see our house. My poor Mother had to go up those stairs to the bedroom to wave out the window to me and blow kisses. If I couldn't see her, I would run home, terrified she had died. It was a worrying time, and Mom had done her best to reassure me. When I think about her having to go up those stairs with her leg spasms, after just having recovered, my heart breaks.

Only a Mother would push through her pain to comfort her child. Thankfully, I did eventually relax, and finding notes in my lunchbox from Mom would help me get through the day.

Julie was nine years older than me, and when I was in school, she and Mom would spend time together. They would spend the day venturing to new places. Mom loved these adventures and often laughed when thinking back. One such day, they got lost in a small Massachusetts town. Julie pulled into a chained linked lot to turn around, a large brick building set back in the lot. Within moments, there were hundreds of children surrounding the car. Mom and Julie sat and laughed when they realized they had pulled into a school play area and the children were in the middle of a religious festival. That day was one of those memories Mom would laugh about for years.

Summer evenings often found us at Peabody Beach. Mom would fill a cooler with sandwiches or cold chicken. We'd have Kool-Aid and chips from a bag. Our plates were full, and we'd sit and enjoy the warm summer sun on our backs, the breeze in our hair, and the sound of the hungry gulls in the distance.

After waiting a half hour, because we had eaten(that's what one did in those days), we would jump in the water or skip rocks with Dad. I loved those evenings.

One summer day, the blimp was coming. We could hear the familiar sound of the engine, and we'd yell," Mom! The blimp is coming!" but, on this particular day, Mom grabbed all the sheets out of the linen closet. We stood by watching her in amazement as she formed the word, Hi, with the sheets on the ground below in our backyard. We waited for the Blimp, and as it moved over us, we waved our hands while jumping up and down, yelling, "Hey, Hey, down here!" Then, the pilot stuck his arm out the window and waved down to us. We were all so excited. Mom waved hello and shouted thank you to the pilot. She laughed and laughed and was so excited that her sign was a success and that we were so happy. What a great day to remember. Summer was in full swing, with many fun-filled days.

One day, while Dad was working his summer job, Mom took us for a ride. It was an overcast day, and that had made for choppy waters. Living on an Island surrounded by water, we were never far from the oceanfront. Mom took us for a ride in the old blue station wagon. We headed around Ocean Drive, a five-mile, oceanfront, scenic ride. The waves would often crash close to the retaining walls along the side of the road. This day was particularly stormy, and Mom noticed the waves were a bit more than she bargained for. We passed by a bend in the road when WHOOSH! Giant waves crashed over the car! The whitewash covered the front window, while the sounds of the windshield wipers, frantically clearing the water, could be heard. We all shouted with fear and surprise, and Mom kept moving. Once we reached a safe place far enough from the crashing waves, Mom breathed a sigh of relief. We were all giddy, but Mom said, "Oh dear, don't tell Daddy he'd be upset to think we could have taken that chance." When we arrived home, Mom decided to let Dad hear about our exciting adventure. He was relieved we were alright but made Mom promise not to go around the drive again on such a stormy day. Mom assured Dad she had no plans to repeat that! In her later years, we would often refer to that day, laughing, she would shake her head, and tsk tsk tsk, saying, "Oh, when I think of it, can you imagine? I'll never forget that day." When Dad worked for the moving company during the summers when he wasn't teaching, he'd bring home huge boxes for us kids. The refrigerator boxes were the best. Ken and I would open these boxes and attach them to make long tunnels in the basement. We'd crawl through them for hours, talking to each other on our soup can phones, connected by a piece of string. "Hello? Can you hear me? Over and Out." We would use the leftover boxes as a sled and slide down the stairs. We'd hit the furnace coil at the bottom of the stairway, in the basement, much to Dad's distress, and Mom would come running, insisting we stop our new dangerous activity. Needless to say, that didn't last long.

Day Trips were always a treat. We would go to the zoo or Charlestown for the day. We'd go to Burlingame State Park, swim, and have a cookout. The tall, dense trees surrounding us always made me feel like we were camping. After a full day of fun, we'd always stop at the Charleston Gift Barn. A large, deep red barn-shaped building filled with the best gifts. Old-fashioned candy, animal figurines, candles, and toys. We loved this place and always came out with goodies that Mom and Dad would buy us to make the day more memorable. Day trips to Galilee were also something to look forward to.

We'd go to the clam shacks and get lunch. The smell of fish and clam cakes, hot crispy french fries sprinkled with malt vinegar, and ketchup, made our mouths water. To this day, I can't be by the water or a pier without thinking about those hot, crispy fries and the smell of vinegar and ketchup.

A fun memory that stands out was a large tuna they had caught at the pier during our visit. We stood nearby, as the big fish was hoisted, by a large crane-like machine. I was young, so this made a lasting impression. For years, I always thought it had been a shark. The gift shops located in the fishing villages were filled with fishing nets in fun colors that you could put in your room, plastic shark toys, and white rope braided bracelets. We wanted it all, of course, and were able to pick out a souvenir from our fun day. On the way home on one of those trips, Julie decided she wanted the bright green fishing net as well, but being too far away by then, they couldn't turn back, and this found Julie disappointed. At a later time, after discussing it with Mom, Dad drove back to buy her that net! What a surprise! I'm not sure what Ken got, but my bet was candy or a shark souvenir. One of my favorite memories was the Indian Pow Wow we attended. The Native American Indians danced to their tribal music in full costume, and I sat watching wide-eyed.

The ceremonies were captivating, and when it was over, we shopped for all the local crafts made by the tribal folks. I remember picking out a beaded necklace with a beaded Indian girl pendant. Oh, how I loved that day. Plymouth Plantation was a trip to remember. We explored the plantation and toured the boats. We walked through the town and had lunch at a park with a small creek running through. I remember Ken and I had Converse sneakers on. He loved those sneakers, and since he wore a large size, that made them hard to find. That day, Ken and I were fussing at each other as siblings do. I was about seven years old, and he was eleven. Mom and Dad were doing their best to keep us apart and hoping that this nagging of one another would stop. Suddenly, I pushed Ken into the creek. That didn't go over too well, and Mom and Dad were not pleased with me. I remember feeling bad as we walked along the street to find a store that would carry new sneakers for Ken so we could finish our day.

Punishment as children was never physical. Mom was big on making us apologize and explaining what we had done. It was important to her to make us understand what we should have done and to know why we were being punished.

We would have to go home and sit in our rooms
until we knew what we did wrong. We'd call out,
"Mom, can I come out yet? I'm sorry." She would
reply, "You have to stay in your room until you know
what you did was wrong," Eventually, she'd come into
the room and sit down. She would put her arms around
us and talk us through our wrongdoings. It always
ended with a kiss, so the punishment wasn't harsh. It
was fair and kind, but she stood by it and didn't give in
until we had understood our behavior.

Summers were short in New England but could get
quite hot, and we started begging for a pool. Mom and
Dad were in their early forties, and they both agreed a
pool would be most enjoyable. Mom and Dad
researched, and after much thought and consideration,
they agreed on getting a pool! Safety was the biggest
concern for my parents. Some pools had deep ends, and
some had one depth. Mom insisted on the pool with
one consistent depth, as she was frightened of someone
losing their footing in the deep end. So it was decided.
An above-ground large rectangle-shaped pool was the
one they chose. It had an aluminum deck wrapped
around it, stairs up, and a ladder. Soon, the backyard
was busy with large machinery hauling away dirt.

Truckloads of sand were delivered and filled the giant hole in the middle of the backyard. Once the landscape was ready to receive the pool, the crew arrived to assemble the large pieces. Mom and Dad picked a pretty blue pebbled liner and blue indoor and outdoor carpeting for the aluminum decking. The metal fencing went up around the decking, and the pool pump was put in place.

Soon, the beautiful new pool stood proudly in the backyard. Mom and Dad would go to the local pool store, where we would pick out loungers to float on and many fun floaties for us kids to enjoy. A basketball net added hours of fun. Dad installed outdoor flood lights, and Mom picked out tiki torches to go around the pool. Mom and Dad named the pool, "What Luck" after a funny commercial they had seen. A picture of them floating in their loungers captured the memory of the first swim. Wow! We were thrilled with this new beauty and took advantage of the crystal-clear aqua-blue water daily. That summer, evenings were spent, with the spotlights illuminating the pool water. The night air was cool, and we kept our shoulders under the water to keep warm and avoid mosquitoes from the field behind the house. Tiki torches were found to be a great mosquito deterrent while creating an inviting ambiance, so it now felt like a tropical hideaway. Dad kept the pump going and skimmed the pool daily of leaves and debris. Mom was diligent about conducting chemical tests on the water every few days, to keep the chlorine and Ph levels safe. They were proud of their pool and wanted to make it safe, for all who wanted to take a dip, as Mom would often say. A sign that said no jumping was the first thing you saw before entering, and the rules of the pool sign also hung nearby. No one was ever allowed to swim alone, a rule Mom made and never broke for the forty-one years the pool remained open. Many happy moments were shared in that pool, birthday parties, family, and laughter. When we were grown with our babies, the children adored swimming in the pool. It was such a treat. Felicia and I spent hours, and hours, year after year, as did my parents, swimming in the pool. My sister's daughter and husband would splash around, enjoying the summer sun. My brother's boys, Caleb and Colby, exhausted themselves as Ken threw them up in the air, and they splashed down. Oh, what fun the pool had provided.

Christmas, as children, was another magical time. In December, Mom would get a call that the catalog was in, and we would jump in the car for the exciting ride to Sears, just down the street. We would hurry down the stairs, and Mom would go to the counter. The lady would reach down and hand Mom the thick catalog with Santa on the front cover. This moment was more exciting than the rest of the year. It was the Sears Christmas catalog, and we were in our glory. We would argue over who could look at it first, and Mom would intervene. Mom would make sure we all got a chance to stare at the pages filled with all the toys that we could hardly wait to receive. We'd circle the toys, and Mom would take notice, making mental notes and lists. I remember sitting under the hooded hair dryer, getting my hair dried, and searching those pages for dolls and accessories. Those were special days. Mom would sit with us on the couch in the evening as we eagerly showed her our wishes in the wish book. Mom and Dad would get busy fulfilling all our lists for Santa in the spirit of Christmas. Just across the shopping center, Santa would visit with his reindeer, yes, real reindeer. They were in large enclosures, and you could feed them hay.

The fact that we were able to feed, real reindeer was an amazing experience and positively magical, and will always be a part of my Christmas memories.

One Christmas, Dad went to New York with a friend to find a doll I wanted. The doll was a doll that was hard to find. Mom pleaded with Dad to find this doll I wanted so badly. Dad searched all the stores in New York City. He looked up and down the shelves until one day he spotted the familiar pink polka-dotted pajamas the doll was wearing, 'There it is !!!" He thought. Dad entered the store in a hurry, only to find that it was the light-skinned version of the doll. "No, that won't do." He would tell the salesman, who looked confused, "But sir, this is the doll everyone wants,"

"Yes, but you see, she is two, and she already has the light-skinned version, and now, she wants the dark-skinned version." Sad and feeling defeated, Dad walked away. It was nearing the end of the day when Dad entered another store, and lo and behold, there it was!!!! Dad quickly asked the salesman to get the doll down from the shelf and called Mom to tell her that he had found it! Mom was thrilled that I would get my little doll, and I was one happy little girl. For many years we would go to the local nursery and pick out the perfect tree. Some years, we would pick out a tall, perfectly shaped tree, other years, a lovely, round, full tree. Dad would put it in the back of the old blue station wagon and bring it into the house. He'd place it in the red metal tree stand, and let it rehydrate, filling the stand reservoir with water. Once satisfied the tree was hydrated and the needles were not shedding, we could start the decorating. The lights were always untangled and strung by Mom and Dad. The blue, green, red, and gold lights twinkled on the tree. In the seventies, the bulbs were larger and gave off a bright warm light. Dad would bring the box of ornaments up from the basement and Mom would carefully unpack the delicate and fun ornaments she had wrapped up the previous January after the Christmas season had passed. The date was always January 6th, The Feast of Little Christmas.

The tree would remain until that day, and Mom would have it no other way. We would all take turns hanging the ornaments until the tree was full of memorable decorations. The gold garland was wrapped around the tree, and the fun part was still to come, tinsel!! We would throw it on the tree just like Mom and Dad taught us. A flick of the wrist and sideways toss usually made for a nice landing, the tinsel perfectly draped over the pine branches. Some tinsel tossings could get messy, and clumps of tinsel sat bunched on the very edge of the branches. Mom would gather the bunch, casually and quietly separating the strands and placing them on the bare branches. Dad would get the spinning light projector set up, and once plugged in, the rotating disc of multiple colors would go around and around, filling the room with the warm lights of Christmas. When it was all finished, I remember laying on my back and looking up into the tree, eyes squinting, making the lights appear like a kaleidoscope. The manager was set up, hay placed, and the cradle left empty until Christmas day. The birthday of baby Jesus. Christmas Eve was always magical, as we were always allowed to open one present from Mom and Dad. Mom would play Christmas carols on the piano, and we'd all sing along. Before we went to bed, we always left carrots and cookies for Santa and his reindeer. One year Dad made reindeer noises on the roof, I was so excited. The joy in those moments was immeasurable. Sometimes, we would go to the five o'clock mass, and sometimes, we would go to the noon mass on Christmas day. The one thing you could count on was hearing my Mother's powerful, beautiful voice filling the very church she grew up attending. Churchgoers would turn around to see where that heavenly voice was coming from, but she would keep singing. Some folks would approach her after mass and compliment her on her voice, and she'd shyly thank them for being so kind.

We would go home and get out of our church clothes to play with our new toys. On the rare occasion that we could not attend church due to weather or illness, Mom would have us read a verse from the Bible. Satisfied, we could then open our presents. Mom always emphasized that Santa was the "spirit of Christmas." She always made sure we knew the real meaning of Christmas. Christmas morning always started with my brother coming into my room saying, "Wee ohh Jennifa Santa Claus came." I'd jump out of bed and run into the living room. We would sit and stare at the tags to see what presents were for us and make noise in the hope Mom and Dad would wake. If they didn't wake, we stood outside their door until they felt our presence. Groggily, they would wake and walk out to the kitchen, and the smell of coffee would soon fill the air. Mom and Dad would call upstairs to wake Julie, and she would come down in her red and white robe. Once we were all together, we could start opening our presents. Crumpled gift wrap and bows were tossed into the large, black garbage bag while Mom took pictures of her children happily opening their gifts. Dad would reach into the bag and retrieve the bows to save them for next year while Mom started breakfast. What a time. There will never be a time like it, ever again. Those days were the days of pure happiness.

Being sick was a great memory. How? You may be wondering. Well, Mom made it that way. On mornings that found us too ill to go to school, there was nothing better than Mom taking our temperature and saying," Well, you're staying home today," The dimly lit room was peaceful, and we were comforted knowing that a day with Mom was ahead. Mom would fill the vaporizer, and the soothing hum of the warm, moist air filled the room. Snug in our bed, Mom would come into our room and place a cold face cloth on our forehead to bring the fever down. She'd give us St. Joseph's aspirin and then sit bedside, rubbing our hair back, singing softly until we fell asleep.

When we started to feel better, Mom would bring in the white bed tray and set up the tray over our laps. We'd sit up, with moist hair from our fever-breaking and wet face cloths. With flushed cheeks and tired eyes, we tried to find the energy to eat. Campbell's chicken soup with stars would be placed on the tray, a plate with saltine crackers on the side, a napkin, and ginger ale with a straw. After dinner, Mom would run to Woolworths with Julie, leaving Dad to watch us so she could get us a special treat. Big thick crayons and coloring books. Colorforms, and Paper dolls. Magic drawing boards and sticker books. When we started to feel better, we'd beg for french fries and a chocolate milkshake. If you could keep it down, this would mean you were on the mend, and we were eager to try. These days were the best, with the warmest, most fulfilling memories. Mom always said, " I think I made it too nice for you kids when you were sick because you never wanted to go back to school."

CHAPTER 8

Daddy

Gramps was a kind, gentle man. He loved his girls and adored his wife. When the children cried at night, they would call for Daddy, and Gramps would come in and sing to them or tell them stories. Mom loved his voice and his soft, calming demeanor. Cyril was a very handsome man with Paul Newman looks and sang well enough to have been noticed. Perhaps this is where Mom got her beautiful voice. He was a man with class, and dressed up he looked very distinguished. Losing Theresa was devastating to Cyril, so his girls would keep him company, take him out, or invite him to their homes. It was a terrible time for him, losing the love of his life so suddenly. Cyril cherished Theresa dearly, but he handled it with grace.

When Gramps had the stroke, it was severely debilitating, but he never lost his sense of humor. He laughed a lot, just like Mom, but his laugh was a quiet, raspy laugh, the kind of laugh that was very contagious.

When Gramps laughed, we all laughed hard. He was an intelligent man and loved good grammar. He taught Mom woodworking skills, and she knew her way around tools. She loved having those skills and often put them to good use around the house, much to my Dad's surprise. She would always give the credit to Daddy. Always the joker, we thought he was hysterical, and the more he joked, the more we laughed. Mom called her Father Daddy, and their favorite song was, "There's no pal in the world like my Daddy," often sung together. Mom had nothing but fond memories of this lovely man.

He was a retired, proud marine who worked at a prestigious private school, St Georges, where he was a bookkeeper. He was good at his job and very well respected. After Mom's illness, when Gramp had to go live with my other aunts, we missed him terribly, especially Mom. He would come to visit, and we all looked forward to seeing him, and we never wanted to let him go. Close to eighty years old now, Gramp also had a pacemaker, had lost the use of one side, and was using a wheelchair, but was still mentally sharp for a man who had suffered a significant stroke some twenty years before. While Mom was recovering, Gramp lived downtown with my other Aunt in the house he owned, the same home where he raised his family. Gramp was relatively healthy but occasionally was hospitalized for minor health issues. One time, in particular, stands out as a fond memory.

It was Christmas time, and Gramp would miss Christmas at home. We visited him every chance we could at the hospital. Mom bought a small tabletop Christmas tree with miniature ornaments and lights. We brought it in and set it up. I can still see him as we decorated the tree, and when we plugged it in, the colorful glow of red, green, and gold sparkled beautifully, filling the room with Christmas cheer. He was thrilled. Gramp's beautiful sea-glass blue eyes filled with tears, and he was beaming with happiness. Gramps was an emotional man, who had no qualms about wearing his feelings on his sleeve, and Mom was just like him.

I remember that day like yesterday. I am so glad we had that moment together. Mom couldn't do enough for her Father and always took the time to make him smile. Gramps loved opera music and appreciated Pavarotti, so Mom ordered a book all about the famed opera singer. She spoke to him early in the morning and said she would like to bring him a surprise later, after lunch. By now, Gramps had a nurse at home, during the day, caring for him. He loved her, and she loved him back, after all, Gramps was easy to love, being so gentle and kind. Mom was getting ready to bring him the book and was looking forward to his reaction, as she knew he would enjoy this gift. The phone rang, and Mom answered cheerfully, as always. She was shocked to hear that it was the doctor, calling to say Gramps had passed away.

She couldn't believe it and told the doctor he must be mistaken, as she had just spoken with him earlier. She sat down, hung up the phone, and sobbed. My brother was home and rushed to her side, comforting Mom in this heart-wrenching moment.

I came home soon after and found Mom in tears. Hearing the sad news, we were all crying and knew Dad needed to come home immediately. I went to the high school where Dad taught and told him Gramps was gone. Dad didn't skip a beat. He quickly locked up his classroom, gathered his things, and left to get home. Dad would spend the evening comforting Mom through her heavy grief. The funeral was beautiful, and Gramps looked so handsome and peaceful. Mom was pleased to see he looked so good, as she had learned that he had received chest compressions in his final moments. The thought upset Mom greatly, and it pained her heart to think of them physically performing life-saving treatments. He was her Daddy, always gentle, never a mean day in his life, and now he had a medical team using extreme measures to bring him back. Mom would have given anything to save her father, but she loved him too much to imagine such harsh measures. This was selfless love, true love, and no one deserved it more than Gramps. The days that followed were filled with sorrow and Mom crying on the couch. Her sobs broke my heart as she missed her Daddy greatly. We did all we could to console her, but only time would comfort her.

The greater the love, the greater the grief. Grief has no timeline, and it's not something you get over. Love has no end. She would love her Daddy forever and hold him in her heart with the sweetest memories.

CHAPTER 9

Changes

Julie was dating and, after a long courtship, was engaged. Ken was in a band. He loved music and playing the electric guitar with his band in the basement. Mom and Dad didn't mind the band playing downstairs. Electric guitars, singing, and amplifiers were booming and banging in the cellar many a night. He shared in the love of music, just like Mom. He was the only one of us that played the piano. Mom tried to teach her girls, but we couldn't get the hang of it. I love to sing, but ironically, when Mom would sing to me as a baby, I was the only one to take my little hands and put them over her face and say, in a tiny voice," Don't sing." Mom would say to Dad, "Isn't she funny? She doesn't want me to sing." I still have no answer for this as I loved it when she sang to me. These are some of my fondest memories, but when I sing now, I can hear her voice in my voice. I don't have the opera quality, but occasionally I can hear her come through.

It was 1977, and Julie was married, so it was now just the four of us at home. Dad is teaching at the local High School, and we were all growing up. Mom was never bored, always happy, and kept busy doing charity work, collecting for organizations, helping the less fortunate, volunteering at hospital gift shops, teaching religious classes, and baking for school events. She could sew clothing like a professional seamstress, knit, crochet, and needlepoint. She took professional cake decorating and produced beautiful wedding cakes and anniversary cakes. She loved the challenge and always met it. She crafted floral arrangements, and if it was out there, she could do it and do it well. She was incredibly multi-talented.

If we failed while trying to follow in her footsteps, she would say, "Don't worry, you tried. You have your talents, you'll see. When you love something and want to do it, you'll do it, and do it well." "You'll discover your talents, maybe things I can't do."

Mom was always the biggest cheerleader, and always made us feel strong and capable of anything. As teens, we all were good kids and never had any trouble. Don't get me wrong, we were teens, and we tested our limits. All in all, we stayed out of trouble. Mom was proud of the family she and Dad raised. With all the struggles along the way, they were looking forward to retirement and rest. Retirement, yes, rest, well… not exactly. Ken was now of the age that he was eager to get out on his own, and he soon packed up and moved to Florida. Mom was sad to see him go but understood Ken needed to spread his wings and explore. Ken never did well sitting in one place very long. Ken did well in Florida, but being a guy, he would check in less frequently than Mom desired, but when he did, Mom would ask if he needed anything.

Mom was known for her Chocolate chip cookies, made from scratch. We grew up with plenty of chocolate chip cookies, a favorite for sure! After chatting with Ken, Mom would start baking. She'd make a few dozen chocolate chip cookies, buy a plastic container big enough to contain them, and place them in a box of packing peanuts with whatever else she thought he needed.

Ken loved getting his care packages from Mom and was always thrilled to find those chocolate chip cookies, a sweet reminder of Mom and home. November was time for Ken's birthday. Mom would bake a cake and freeze it. She'd wrap the cake in tin foil and place the icing in a container with candles and supplies needed for a birthday party. She would bring the finished package to the post office, mark it fragile, and send it off to Florida, with hopes it would arrive intact. Lo and behold! It always arrived in one piece! Ken, thrilled to find his Birthday in a box, would assemble his cake, lovingly baked by his dear Mother.

Mom never skipped a beat with us. She always wanted her children to know how much she cared about them. When I had moved away for a short time, Mom never missed a day of writing me letters. The highlight of my days was going to my mailbox and seeing those letters sent from home. She would fill me in on everything happening back home, and, in turn, I'd write back updating her on what was happening to me. I missed being home so very much, but my then-husband was in the service and we were transferred to Maryland, then Virginia. Thankfully, this was just a year, but a very long year indeed.

Julie had exciting news. She was expecting her first baby with her husband. Mom and Dad were thrilled, and this meant Mom had shopping to do. Mom loved a well-dressed baby, so she and I would go to Amy Jane's on Bellevue Avenue, an upscale baby boutique that sold beautiful baby clothes. Mom was a talented seamstress. She appreciated beautiful clothing and she was in her glory. Knowing it was a boy, Mom would go through the clothing on delicate hangers, piece by piece. Only the best would do, and she had exquisite taste.

One by one, beautiful rompers with smocks were placed on the counter. Mom knew just what to look for. She'd pick up an article of clothing and say," Now, this is a beautifully made piece," Look at those seams," Mom was big on seams. She would often say that the clothing she made could be worn, inside out because of those beautiful seams. Soon, the bags are filled with crisp white, light blue, tiny outfits with trucks and puppies. Our hands full, we carry the bags swinging gently, as we walk along Bellevue Avenue to our car. Excitement filled the air for the new baby to arrive, and Mom was delighted. One thing about Mom was her positivity. You could feel it.

She was contagious. I was always so impressed by that. All three of us children had different personalities. Julie was quiet and reserved, very much like Dad. Ken was energetic and musically inclined but a free spirit. I was a puzzle, cautious but bold, mellow but loud, and sweet but fresh. We are still very much the same, though not one of us as unique as Mom. Being a Nana came easy to Mom. Baby Matthew arrived, and he was everything we imagined him to be. Julie was an RN, and her husband also worked. So, Mom offered to care for Matt full time and loved it. Days were filled with lullabies and walks in the pram, the old-fashioned carriage on giant wheels with springs and a canopy. It looked like royalty, and we all had been an occupant of its regalness at one time or another. Inside, the pram was dressed with beautiful linens and handmade white afghans, the lap of luxury. People would stop and admire the baby as Mom walked along, singing and smiling, in the warm sun. Mom believed that babies needed fresh air and sunshine, so if she could get out for a walk, she would. At home, she rocked him to sleep, singing softly of, "Denim and dump trucks, Oh where have they gone?" "Turn around and your two, turn around and your four, turn around, and you're a young man walking out the door."

Needless to say, Mom loved being a Nana. Soon, we were saddened to learn that baby Matthew had a hole in his heart, so they traveled to Rhode Island Hospital for testing. We were all terribly worried. Mom and Dad accompanied my sister to Providence while they put baby Matthew into a tube to X-ray his little heart. In the meantime, while waiting for test results, he was to be kept warm and not get a cold, as it was February and the days were frigid. Julie's husband, at that time, was hot-blooded and insisted on having an air-conditioner and a fan in the heart of winter. While Julie worked as an RN during the early shift, her husband had weekends off, and Matthew would stay with his father. Like any new Mom, Julie would call home to check on the baby, only to hear the fan and air-conditioner running in the background. Julie would insist that he turn it off, but he would assure her the baby was in his snowsuit, in the bassinet, nice and warm. Well, that wasn't going to fly well with Julie. Julie would call Mom and Dad and ask if we could go out and get the baby. The ride was twenty minutes, and we were happy to do it. So, without question or weather conditions, we would jump into the blue Toyota and take a ride to get the baby.

We'd arrive and gather up baby Matthew to take him to Nan and Pops. Julie would call, and Mom would reassure her the baby was now with them, and Julie could continue her work day in peace.

That's what being grandparents is all about, being there when the parents can't be. Eventually, baby Matthew's hole in his heart closed, and Julie divorced shortly after. She moved home with the baby, and we were all thrilled. Julie continued her job as a registered nurse at the local hospital, and we spoiled Matthew and loved it. Three years passed, Julie remarried, I married, and my brother married. Shortly after, the children started to arrive, one after another, but Nana and Pop's arms were open and ready for more babies to love.

CHAPTER 10

Grandparenting

If you were a baby, these are the arms you'd want to hold you. This was the voice you'd love to hear singing you to sleep. This was safety, this was contentment. Matthew, now four, thrived in all this loving care and loved to go outside with Poppa and water the garden. He was a big helper, and Pop couldn't be any happier. Matt spent many an evening on Pop's lap, watching National Geographic. He loved his Nana and Papa, and they adored spending quality time with their boy.

In 1987, I got the exciting news that I was pregnant, and in November 1988, a sweet, blonde-haired, blue-eyed baby girl was born. Nana and Poppa rushed to the hospital in the middle of the night to welcome their beautiful new granddaughter, Felicia Marie Victoria, named after Nana and me. Mom asked the nurse, "Is she as beautiful as I think she is?" The nurse replied, "Contrary to all belief, not all newborns are beautiful, but this one is." Felicia arrived home to thrilled, nervous new parents, but Nana reassured them that it was all under control.

Nana dove right in, sharing all her knowledge, advising us what to worry about and what not, and, of course, getting in on all the snuggles she could in between. Two grandchildren, one boy, and one girl, how blessed they felt. Victoria and Bill were so proud when showing off their little ones. Matthew, now age five, and baby Felicia had their hearts. Grandparenting wasn't always easy. Matt had a hole in his heart, and although closed, Nana still watched closely, but Matt was usually right on Pop's heels, so that made the job a little easier.

Felicia was a quiet baby and not in a hurry to crawl. This concerned Nana, but being such a passive little one, Nana thought she'd wait it out. When babysitting, Nana loved to talk to her babies. She would say, "Tell me a story," and the babies would coo away, little legs and arms moving in conversation, and of course, she would sing. The babies listened intently. Felicia was an early talker but not an early walker, and now Nana's concerns were rising. Nana voiced her concerns to me.

The baby should be holding her bottle or reaching for rattles. Nervously, I took my baby to the pediatrician, who assured me that Felicia was just a lazy baby. This concerned Nana, but time would tell. At eighteen months old, Felicia was cherub-like, with curly blonde hair, blue eyes, and big chubby round cheeks. She was talking, but she wasn't walking or crawling. She substituted crawling for a funny and very fast bunny hop, as we called it. She could stand and hold on and was into everything, but independent walking was not on her radar. During her well-baby visit, the doctor's eyebrows finally raised. He examined her and said all was fine again, a lazy baby, but lazy, she wasn't. Baby Felicia got around very quickly, but walking was a long way off, it would seem.

One day, I received a call from the pediatrician to bring Felicia in and to bring someone with me. This thought frightened me, and Nana's heart sank. Nana and Pop accompanied me with the baby. We arrived at the doctor's office. Dad chose to wait outside, as his nerves had the best of him. Nana came in with me and the baby. We walked into a room with chairs set up so that the doctor sat facing us, and we the pupils. We were terrified. The doctor started speaking.

" Well, you know you've had concerns, and so have I. I believe her skull has stopped growing and that this may be the start of a long dark road, in which there will be more valleys than peaks." I spoke up and said, "I asked you if she was okay, I spoke of my concerns, and you assured me she was fine," his response was, "Well, listen, we all want perfect houses, perfect cars, perfect kids, and well, sometimes it doesn't happen" At this point Nana intervenes, and not quietly.

Normally very poised and polite, Nana unleashed her absolute disbelief on the doctor. "How dare you! How dare you compare my granddaughter to a house or car! My daughter would sleep in a box if it meant her daughter was okay." The doctor was left speechless and had no explanation. When asked why he waited when we had voiced our concerns, he said, "Well, I suspected something was wrong, but didn't know what it was." No, he didn't know. He didn't know a thing, it seemed. Being Felicia's Mommy, I asked the question that I feared most. "Is she going to die?" The doctor answered, "She may," It was at **this moment** that I found myself on the other side of the room. I can see myself and my Mother with the baby on her lap and the doctor in front of us.

A nurse walked by but didn't notice me, and just as fast as that happened, I was back in my body, staring at my Mother's now, huge green eyes staring back at me, asking, "What just happened?" and then, the tears, tears, and tears. I can't explain what happened that day, but I do know that stress can kill you, and if I hadn't experienced it myself, I would find it hard to believe. I think the thought of losing my child, literally sent my soul out of my body to ease the pain of such a thought. We left the office, and upon seeing me upset, Dad asked Mom what happened. She whispers, "Don't ask, it's not good. I'll tell you later." The ride home was quiet except for my crying. As soon as we enter the house, my Mother gets on the phone with the best-known local pediatrician and sets up an appointment. After much discussion with the nurse, we felt like she had made some headway. Mom assured me we'd get through this. Although she couldn't walk, she had a lot going for her and seemed normal in every other way. You may wonder why I am telling you family stories, but I want to share the powerful impact that Mom and Dad made in our journey. Victoria was a force to be reckoned with, especially when it came time for her babies, and her grandchildren were no exception. I trusted her completely and leaned on her so much during this very dark time. Not only did she support me, but she became our best therapist, interventionist, and cheerleader. After all, this is Mom, and I told you she was something else, an angel sent to earth, and we were just the lucky ones. The visit to the new doctor proved to hold a lot of hope. He looked over the baby and said, "This baby deserves a second look."

The doctor agreed that she had a lot going right for her, and she was strong in many aspects but weak in others. She's a puzzle," he said," but I'm going to go out on a limb and tell you that I don't think she is going to die, and I do believe that it's muscular." He referred us to Rhode Island Hospital's top neurologist and team.

CHAPTER 11

Fighting for Felicia

Nana and Papa accompanied us to Rhode Island Hospital. We are seen, by a large team, of pediatric specialists. One appointment, after another, all day long, until the entire pediatric team had examined her. The physical therapist discussed the possibility of cerebral palsy and muscular dystrophy. The neurologists discuss brain tumors and worse. To say it was terrifying was an understatement. So far, the one thing they all agree on now is that she will not die, but may need leg braces and therapy. MRI scans, CAT scans, PET scans, and ultrasounds. MRIs with contrast, X-rays, and blood work were all very traumatic for a baby, and the three of us watching and waiting were terrified. Sedating an almost two-year-old is not easy. Holding her down for blood work would sometimes take three men, as she was so strong and would fight so hard. Every muscle in her body tightly flexed as she screamed and tightened up to avoid that needle. The ride home was one hour long, and poor Felicia would just shutter after all that trauma, as she tried to stop crying, her body jumping with every breath, trying to regain composure. Nana held her over her car seat, wrapping her arms around her, caressing her head, and singing to her in between." Shh, shh, shh, relax, it's okay, it's all over." Finally, completely exhausted, she would fall asleep as I drove home through heavy traffic with a broken heart. Dad sat up front, concerned. My heart shattered, tears running down Mom's cheeks. We all felt her pain and wanted it to stop.

MRIs with contrast aren't easy. It's a dye they inject for a better visual. Felicia would suffer headaches as a side effect, and she would vomit heavily all the way home. These appointments were hard on her and all of us. When your child is ill, you would give your right arm to make them well. After months and months of grueling testing, sitting amongst the sickest of children, and wondering about your child's fate, we finally were able to be seen by the top neurologist.

He was Indian and seemed a bit stoic, to say the least. He also appeared he was not one to question, but we were not ones to be quiet either, so we trod lightly. He examined the baby. Test after test, measurements, and questions. He put her on the floor, held up toys, and on and on it went.

The doctor sat quietly, writing his notes intently, and finally looked at us and said, quite strictly, "This child has no spasticity. Some muscles are strong, some muscles are weak." "She has a muscle imbalance. She will need physical therapy." "She will walk." We were stunned! It was said, with such conviction, that we believed him.

It was as though we stood before Jesus himself at that moment, as he delivered the best news possible, and we were thrilled and shocked. "Really?" We asked, "She's not going to die?" "She doesn't have cerebral palsy?" "She doesn't have a brain tumor?" He shook his head no to all of those. God had sent a miracle, and we felt like we were dreaming. We were so thankful. The very stoic doctor smiled at our grateful reaction toward him. Thank you, God! We left the hospital that day, with renewed hope and hearts full of joy. It was like giving birth to her all over. Wow, wow, wow!

Mom cried, and we all hugged! Dad was thrilled, and we happily drove home, and couldn't wait to share the news.

Perhaps by now, you are wondering where my husband is. I didn't want to waste one page on him, but he didn't want to be involved. One of the doctors said he was out in left field, and he proved himself to be just that. That's another story, but I'll leave it as we divorced, and he was never involved ever again, not in any way. He walked away from his wife and sick baby and never looked back. Therapy started in our town in our local hospital, and Felicia was making progress. Up and down the stairs, up and down the slide, teeter totters for balance, reaching, stacking, stretching, all part of the day. Once at therapy, an elderly gentleman sat in a wheelchair waiting for his therapy session. Felicia is two years old and calls out to the man." You can't walk?" she asks, "No honey, I'm old, and I can't walk too well," he answered. "I can't eve-a (either)," she replied in her little toddler voice. "But I will pway (pray) for you," she said. The man was shocked! "Oh no, she can't walk?" He asked, "No, but we are working on it," I replied. He waved to Felicia as the therapist arrived for his therapy.

Felicia knew she couldn't walk. She was well aware, accepted it, and prayed for others in her situation, even at the tender age of two. Amazingly dear, and very unusual, and so beautiful to witness

Another time after therapy, while putting her in her car seat, Felicia tells us, "I saw Jesus today." Surprised, we asked, "You did?" "Where?" "In the mirror," she said happily. He said, "Hi, Felicia!" "He was nice." What more could we say? except Jesus was here with us every step of the way.

CHAPTER 12

The Therapist

At twenty-two months, Felicia walked her first steps from Nana to me, and from me to Nana. Sitting on the living room floor, I still hear us cheering," Yay!!!!!! You did it!" Clapping and laughing! I can see it all like it was yesterday. What a miracle that day was, the joy immense. Pop comes into the room to witness it again, and now we are all clapping! I can see Mom's head back laughing with pure joy and Felicia smiling so proudly with those strong, little legs beneath her. This day was perfect! " Praise God through whom all blessings flow," Mom would say. We weren't going to sit back and let nature take its course, no siree, we got busy. Nana, naturally being incredible, had supported us in every way possible. She attended therapy sessions with me, taking it all in, asking questions, and getting involved. By hook or by crook, this baby would be at her best, God willing.

Nana put picnic benches together to create a narrow path. She felt if we brought her legs while attempting to walk, it would help her align while walking. It worked! Felicia was walking with her legs closer together and not so toddler-like. Nana put ankle weights on Felicia and crawled behind her and over while taking Felicia's legs and patterning the crawl. One leg, one arm, another leg, another arm, until a four-point creep was in full gear. It took time, but it happily happened with constant work and determination. The baby was into everything. The terrible twos were in full gear, and we couldn't be happier. We sat for hours with felt board pieces and pictures, quizzing our little toddler. We loved to watch her having so much fun while learning. Felicia was making progress, and we were not going to be deterred. We purchased every fine motor toy. We'd go to the educational stores for specialty toys. I once found a wooden slide at a yard sale, exactly like the one they used in therapy. It had three stairs, with railings on either side and a small sliding board.

I bought it without giving it a second thought. Nothing was too good for my baby. Everything we did for Felicia, was done with therapy in mind and a goal to reach. We would do everything and anything, to get her to where she needed to be. She was **thriving** and was reaching significant milestones!

Soon, Felicia graduated from therapy, but we were armed with all the tools we needed to keep it going at home, and boy, did we. It was a full-time job, and we were all dedicated. I was a single mom now, so I was working full-time as well. Nana and Pop took care of Felicia during the day, and while I missed her terribly, I knew she was in the best hands possible. So naturally, when Nana had the baby all day, she wasn't about to waste that time. Outside on beautiful, warm, sunny days, she would walk behind baby Felicia, as she pushed her wide-spaced, wheeled shopping cart in the grass. This little cart was built with the idea of helping babies walk. Mom would fill it with a five-pound bag of sugar to weigh it down, and Felicia would push. Smiling from ear to ear and falling to her knees, only to get back up to push more to the sound of Nana clapping and yelling, "Whoo hoo, good job, good girl!!!"

We would sing a little song about picking yourself up, brushing yourself off, and starting over again. Encouragement was not scarce. I arrived home to a full report of happy news of the day's accomplishments. What a blessing it was to have such incredible parents, dedicated to the well-being of your child.

Julie soon found she was pregnant with her second child. This pregnancy was fragile, and kept her in bed, on bed rest. Mom bought her needlepoint and crafts to keep her busy and pass the time. We would all go to the house to help with household chores and entertain Matthew. Julie's husband was a firefighter and worked on our side of the bridge, so with Julie in bed, Dad would take the thirty-minute ride over the bridge to pick up Matthew from school. Sadly, at five months along, Julie's water broke, and baby Joshua was too little to survive. While we were all heartbroken, we did our best to support and show comfort to Julie as needed. A year later, Julie's prayers were answered, when she found out she was pregnant again.

This pregnancy also put her on bed rest, however, she welcomed her rainbow baby, Elise, in 1990. After maternity leave and enjoying her new baby girl,

Julie returned to work as a nurse while leaving baby Elise in Nana and Papa's care. Now, there were three little ones in their care, but Matt was in kindergarten for some of the time. There were days I would come home from work to find Felicia in her high chair or booster seat, Elise in her baby seat or swing, and Matt coloring at the table. All three little ones were perfectly content while Nana baked cookies and talked to her grandbabies. What a site!! I will never forget it. I walked in, shocked at the busy scene. "Oh, Hi darling, how was your day?" She would say in a happy, sing-song tone. I asked, "Wow, what is happening here?" She replied, "What?" "We are having a wonderful day. We just had lunch, and now, we are playing, baking, and singing. It's a beautiful day!" This right here, was the perfect picture of who my Mom was. My Mom is an incredibly positive woman who never ceases to amaze me. I wanted to be just like her, but I knew I could never get close to it. She was different, I swear, an angel in disguise. When Felicia ended up getting sicker, I was taking care of a little one in my home, as this enabled me to be home with Felicia. Mom agreed to take this little one under her care to help me out, while I took time out of work, so that I had more time to take Felicia to therapy sessions, and doctor visits. Mom didn't mind having another baby added to the babies in her care, and she seemed to fit right in, and loved Nana and Pop.

We were so fortunate to have parents who took such wonderful care of our children when needed. Julie's daughter Elise, and my daughter were just two years apart. Nana would set up a small pool for them to splash in, play outside, and sit nearby, taking photographs. Many happy days were enjoyed in the backyard, on warm sunny days. Mom and Dad pushing the girls on the swings and watching them play. Mom loved to take pictures of her two granddaughters together, always showing them off, saying, "Aren't they darling?" She was a dedicated Nana, and Dad, a fun-loving Pop. How Mom had all those babies in her care and still managed to help me, was amazing, and I'm still eternally grateful for her strength, and huge heart.

CHAPTER 13

Another Mountain to Climb

Once again, life decided to throw another curve ball our way. It was an ordinary summer day when Mom and I took Felicia, now two, shopping with us. I put her in the cart, and we started to browse. Felicia suddenly grimaced like she was in pain. She made a little scrunched-up face with little grunting noises we had never seen or heard. We immediately addressed her, looking for the reason for her discomfort. While we found no reason for her concerning behavior, and we hoped at best, it may have been gas, as it passed as quickly as it started. It appears she was none the worse for the wear, acting pleasant and enjoying her outing with Nana and Mommy. Soon after, while Julie was visiting, I was holding Felicia on my lap when she did the same peculiar behavior.

"There it is!" We yelled. "That's what she did the
other day!" "What is that?" Julie quietly and reluctantly
said, "I think that's a seizure." "A seizure? "Don't say
that," I was devastated and reduced to tears. I cried, and
cried, that my sweet baby had yet another mountain to
climb. Doctor visits galore, hospitals, and tests lead us
back to Rhode Island Hospital. It was soon determined
that Felicia was having seizures, and the worst kind
was soon to come. When one experiences more than
one seizure, you are diagnosed with Epilepsy. In this
case, there were no findings. No, known cause. MRI,
CAT scans, and EEGs, all said no brain damage. No,
oxygen deprivation. **No** reason. Our little girl, who had
triumphed so well in walking when doctors thought she
might never walk, is now having seizures. One doctor,
in particular, thought he may have an explanation. He
explained," The car in your driveway hasn't started for
some time. It's rusty, but soon after some oil and some
work, the engine starts, but sputters and overheats. The
brain may be doing that in a sense. Felicia didn't walk
on time, but with work we got her moving and now the
brain is making connections it hadn't made before. It
was running now, but not running smoothly." It made
sense, but we never did find its source. It would've
been nice to believe the cute scenario the doctor

painted, however, there was no medical explanation. Little Felicia, now heavily medicated, goes from a gentle toddler to a hyperactive toddler. Some of the anti-seizure drugs cause hyperactivity, and we were now running wild after this very active toddler. There is active, and then there is hyperactive, and we knew we couldn't keep her on this particular medication, as it was changing her drastically. So many medications were tried. Some made her ill, some hyperactive, some found her listless and almost lifeless. Terrified and saddened, appointment after appointment, we all waited with bated breath for a cure. Lullabies and dancing, we comforted our baby as much as possible. Poppa sings and dances with her to "You are my sunshine" as she calms quickly in his safe arms. It takes all three of us onboard, all the time, to comfort her and to get our baby back to feeling like herself. It was hell, but soon my little sweetheart was smiling again. With a significant amount of medication onboard, baby Felicia seems to settle in, and her little personality returns! A much more fatigued toddler, but as charming as ever.

Nana and Pop found Felicia funny, as did I, of course. Not just because I'm her mother, but, because she was funny, and had a way of saying profound things that left us always running around looking for a pen and paper to jot down what she said. I could go on and on, but I'll spare you otherwise, this would be chapters long. A perfect example of her humor is a memory that always leaves us laughing. Felicia had just turned three. Nana and I were at the local hospital with Felicia for her scheduled CT scan. In the early 1990s, the CT scans were done in a large truck that came to the hospital. It entailed loading her into a capsule, of sorts, and closing the large door into the darkness. Nana and Mommy were worried and knew this would be scary for all of us, especially Felicia. Felicia was positioned on the table, and I assured her Mommy and Nana would be right outside the door.

She was loaded into the dark chamber and was instantly terrified. The technician slid the table in, with the touch of a button, as we continued to yell words of encouragement towards our frightened little one. "Mommy, I'm scared!" her little voice echoed in the darkness. The table slides out, and she is immediately covered in kisses and enveloped. "Shh, we're right here. What a big girl! You did it, but now we have to do it, one more time, and we are all done!" "Then we will go get a treat, okay honey?"

I reassured my baby, terrified myself but not letting on. Nana, however, being true to herself, assured her in her own way. "Now, I want you to pray when you are in there. I want you to ask the Blessed Mother to wrap her cloak around you, and ask Jesus to protect you, okay? Can you do that?" The table slides in. We shout more encouragement, and her little voice, from afar, can be heard shaking with fear. Our hearts were breaking when the tech told us, "Okay, we got a clear picture." and slid her out.

We were grateful for the patient technician, and grateful that it was over. As we are putting her little pink Oshkosh winter coat on, Nana asks, "Did you pray?" Felicia replied, in her little toddler voice so sweetly, "Yes I did. I said, "Dear Jesus, get me the hell out of here!" We laughed, and laughed, as Nana winked at me saying, "Well, not exactly what I was hoping, but okay." Oh, how we laughed. This baby certainly had a way with words, and we loved her!

CHAPTER 14

Busy Busy Busy

Years passed with Felicia's seizures under control, and she was flourishing! As usual, Nana's days were busy taking the children to school with Pop, and picking them up for their working parents. When the schools had events that needed baked goods, we would gladly bring in our baked goods, just like Mom had taught us. If we were working late, Mom would surprise us by making them and having them ready when we came to pick up the children after work. Wow, we were always beyond grateful for her thoughtfulness. She loved to help her daughters, who worked all day, and we certainly appreciated everything she did. It would seem that the only time Mom and Dad had time off, was when we picked the babies up after work and headed to our own homes for the evenings.

Life seemed to be coasting along, and Mom decided that she wanted to do something for herself, something she enjoyed doing. Makeup and jewelry were always something Mom appreciated, so she decided to sell Avon. Mom attended weekly meetings, where they would teach them about the products, and folks would share their stories and product information. She loved these meetings and met a friend, Jan. They would sit together and chuckle and get a bite to eat in the restaurant next door occasionally. Soon, Mom was ready to sell on her own. She would order catalogs and samples of makeup and lipstick. Soon, the boxes arrived filled with catalogs, bags, literature, samples, and gifts from time to time.

Mom was so excited. I'd sit with her and help stamp the back of the books with her information for those who wish to place an order. We would leave the catalogs in supermarkets and take them to work, and soon, customer orders were rolling in. The boxes of products would arrive, and Mom would process the orders, adding samples to the bags and new catalogs with new products available. She would load up the car and by appointment, deliver the orders. Some of her customers would ask her in their homes, and Mom would go over the samples with them and take out her lipstick sampler and makeup guides. She adored doing this, and her customers loved her. Meetings were becoming more and more fun, and Mom was selling a lot of products, therefore, she received more fun perks. She'd come home from the meeting excited to tell us all about them and the prizes she received. Mom continued to do this for years until she found that life was starting to feel too busy, and she needed to take a break, so she retired from her much-loved job with a feeling of accomplishment.

When not busy with the children, Victoria spent her days keeping busy. She would organize her fabrics and patterns, work in the basement, box up items, and make large signs to tape on the front to mark the contents. Mom prided herself on her organizational skills and always felt it was a job well done. She could never go a day without completing a task, only then did she feel accomplished. Victoria made clothing, and delicate Afghans covered our babies. She would knit hats for babies and premature babies and donate them to the local hospital maternity ward. Cakes were made and decorated for anniversaries and special occasions, beautiful enough for any bakery or cover of a magazine.

She had taken cake decorating courses, and her skills were that of a professional. If neighbors were ill, she stepped in to provide personal hands-on care or to bring a pan of brownies, cinnamon bread, or cake, always at their door in times of need or grief. Mom would always send cards with words of love and encouragement for all occasions. Oh, how she loved her cards. She even had a drawer all labeled for every occasion, filled with cards just like the greeting card stores. Gift wrap, gift bags, tissue, bows, ribbon, and tape, were all together. If you needed to wrap a gift, she had you covered. Our wedding gowns were beaded by hand, and our Christening gowns were made with matching bonnets. She made bouquets for weddings, guitar covers for my brother, and a graduation gown for Felicia some years later.

Mom was always helping those in need. When a neighbor's son had a stroke, Mom headed right over to her house, up the street, to help her in any way she could. She helped the son get dressed, cared for his wounds, and provided comfort. Mom had watched him grow from a tiny little boy to a grown man. He was no stranger to her, and he loved her. Once he was comfortable, and Mom had addressed his needs, she would help her friend by chatting with her, giving encouragement, cutting her hair, curling it, or setting it to make her feel better.

She wasn't the only neighbor she lovingly cared for. There were many others. She always asked God for guidance, love, and patience, even if it meant going beyond the call of duty and helping in difficult situations. She did her best, and her faith gave her strength. I'm not sure that there was much she couldn't do. Her children reflect her in many ways. Ken plays the piano and the guitar, loves to write, and appreciates good grammar. He shares her likes and dislikes. Julie likes to sew, knit, bake, and do crafts. I bake, crochet, paint, write, and sing. Not one of us can hold a candle to Mom's great array of talents, but we share many similarities. She still amazes me to this day and will forever continue to do so. Sooooo…. Mom could knit, crochet, bake, cook, decorate cakes like a pro, and gift wrap like a high-end boutique. She taught religious instruction, homeschooled, babysat all the children, and sang while doing so. She cared for her elderly father, she was a therapist, crafter, florist, counselor, pianist, vocalist, writer, faithful follower of God, a loving wife, mother, grandmother, daughter, friend, bookkeeper, hairdresser and had an intense need to educate herself and others. She was a class act, a grammar corrector, an avid reader, an enthusiast, and had a great sense of humor.

Faith was the basis for everything Victoria did. The day started with faith and ended with it, never fading and always strong even, in the darkest times. I asked her many times, "How did you get through that ?" or "How did you stay so positive?" and her answer was always the same, "I have my faith. Without it, I would not have made it." She'd say, "Hey, listen, I want to go to heaven someday. I want to be worthy." It was almost as if she was planning the vacation of a lifetime, always planning, always thinking of arriving at the place you can't wait to see. Faith, check..., good deeds, check... Love, check... She's good to go. She never felt she **was** worthy. She only hoped to be **found** worthy. I believe Mom had a few goals in life. Some of these goals were to become a great Mother and for her children to know she loved them. She worked hard to be a good, faithful wife, to do God's work, and to make it home to heaven, worthy of a place in eternity. I could go on forever. She was pretty darn spectacular! Time passes, and so much is accomplished. Julie and her husband have three children. Matthew, from her first marriage, Elise, and baby Joshua in heaven. Ken has two children, Colby and Caleb, and I have Felicia. Dad has retired and is now finally relaxing. All the grandchildren are grown. On days off, Victoria and Bill spend their time busy in the house. Dad loved grocery shopping, getting his bargains, and gardening. Mom stayed busy doing what she did best, spending time with Felicia and keeping busy, organizing, baking, and helping sick neighbors she'd known for years.

Mom would bathe them and help them with dressing. Felicia decided that she'd like to help, so she would accompany Nana, cleaning their homes and helping with the dogs, and in any way she could be of help. Mom never turned away from those in need. She felt she was called by God to do his good work. When those times tried her, she would pray God would give her the strength to get through it. She'd say," I think I earned a star in my book today, only my faith could've gotten me through that." We always would suggest that she hold back a bit and learn to say no while reaching out to others to help, but she continued to move through her comfort zone to help others in any way she could. It pained her to see others in need or pain, so she would do anything to help them. I'm pretty sure Mom's book was filled with stars in heaven.

Mom never swore and hated it when we would. Now she was human and could get angry like anyone else, but it was a rare occasion, she just really appreciated fairness and respect.

If anyone were to take God's name in vain, Mom would always speak up and say, "Blessed be the name of Jesus," every single time. I can't remember a time when it didn't happen. She didn't care if we didn't like being corrected, she'd stand her ground, and it **wasn't** allowed. If the children repeated anything offensive they heard from other children Mom would sing a little song about not swearing to change the course. We'd laugh, but it worked. Mom also taught us not to be envious of others and always reminded us that God had plans, and one never knew what the future held for them. Life was unpredictable and she reminded us of that. She wanted us to stay focused on what we did have, not what we didn't or wanted. If things were unjust, Mom would always say, "God will not be mocked, you mark my words." I'm thankful for those important lessons of wisdom as I often fall back on them to this day, and it has helped me tremendously in difficult times.

CHAPTER 15

Comfort

Comfort, we all need it, especially as children. Mom was exceptional at comforting. I was nine when Mom was so ill with the virus that had attacked her spinal cord, and I was terrified she would get sick again. I was a nervous wreck and worried excessively. Mom took me to the pediatrician, who reassured me and suggested relaxation techniques. It didn't work, so Mom got to work with her own ideas to relieve my stress. She found a paper with a certificate, and on that certificate were pom-pom eyes. The certificate said I'm your worrywart. I worry for you. She used an empty cigar box, covered it with pretty paper, and attached the certificate and pom-pom worrywart to the top. She presented it to me, and of course I laughed. She told me to put all my worries within that box, and that my new worry wart would worry about it for me. With the innocence of a child, I filled that box, and when I closed the lid. I was confident that Worrywart would take care of it for me.

Mom's comfort didn't end there. Many nights, she would sit on our beds, talking with us and guiding us through our teenage years. When shopping, Mom would always come home with a surprise for us, always there for us, always thinking about us. While a Mother's work is never done, her role as a comforter continues strongly in our lives. Our parents were there through divorces, my sister's baby's death, my daughter's illness, and everyday stresses. Mom and Dad didn't skip a beat. Mom's hours and hours of phone calls, advice, and laughter always helped us through. She was always there. She always knew what to say. We were lucky to have parents that never failed us, ever. The comfort she provided never wavered, even in her darkest days. Spoiling Mom was an absolute pleasure. We would go shopping every Wednesday after visiting the Chinese buffet for lunch. Mom would head straight to the jewelry case and necklace area to find a pretty piece. She loved pins and rings and would often surprise us with something pretty that caught her eye. Mom also collected rosary beads. It wasn't something she set out to do, but if she saw a pair, she just couldn't leave them. So, it began. The collection. Mom would buy small pouches with zippers from the purse department to hold the precious finds.

When we arrived home from shopping, she'd put them in a decorative box for safekeeping. She would go through them and say, "When I die, I want you to donate some of these to the hospital chapel." I've yet to do that, but I will be sure to make good on Mom's wishes. I'll write a note to attach in hopes that the person who finds a rosary will know how special Mom was. Hopefully, they will cherish the good and faith in those special beads.

When shopping, my daughter and I would love to find beautiful blouses, blazers, etc., for Mom. My daughter shared the same taste in clothing and always knew just the right piece to buy. Felicia was thrilled at the thought of gifting Nana with these carefully chosen gifts, and we knew she would be most grateful.

After a long day, we would unpack our treasures and glow with satisfied smiles, knowing we had found something special. Mom was so much fun, a total ray of sunshine and positivity. We'd say, "Okay, we have a surprise for you," and she always said, "Oh, you spoil me," and, "I hope you bought something you liked for yourself." We handed her her surprise as she stood smiling, eyes closed, hands out. Once the item touched her hand, she opened her eyes and showed her delight with her beautiful, happy tone, "Oh, so beautiful!" or

"Where did you find this?" Shopping for Mom became a fun adventure for us, as Mom was easy to please. She loved everything, and funny enough, they fit her perfectly every time. She would jokingly say," I never have to shop because I have personal shoppers who pick stylish things, and they fit perfectly." Oh, we would laugh.

Mom collected dolls, and we came across some real finds. She adored them and would find them all just darling. If they needed a makeover, she would delight in using the wig brush she had purchased just for doing the doll's hair, and by the next day, the frazzled-haired, well-loved, or forgotten doll, looked like new in their new clothing and freshly washed hair. Then she'd proudly name it. Oh, what fun we'd have. She was just a joy to surprise, so we did it a lot, but in return, she filled her cart with surprises for us. So, sweet memories were made on those trips. These are memories I will carry with me forever.

Forever, we hear folks say it all the time. We will live here forever, they say when buying a house, or I'll love you forever. I'll be with you forever. What is forever? I don't think here on the earthly side, there is a forever. Forever, only exists in eternity, where there is no end. Here, there is only the present, the here and now. Nothing is ever promised here, in the present. The house you live in will someday be someone else's home. One day, the people you love will pass into another realm and leave us behind grieving. Our possessions will belong to someone else or be thrown away. So what is forever? Forever is the love in our hearts that never changes. Forever is waiting. Forever is the hope, the memories no one can take. Living in the moment is so very important, as it's all we have. Spoil your loved ones, take the trip, and relive those memories.

Life is fragile and fleeting. Hurry....., live it, love it. We don't have much time. Smile, hug, kiss, laugh, and make it count. Make it count.

CHAPTER 16

Getting Older

If nothing else, the numbers were increasing on the birthday cakes. Mom felt well for her age, and as she grew older, she made a conscious effort to maintain her health. She took her meds for her high blood pressure, and Afib, saw her doctors regularly, had blood work, and kept active. As modern science discovered things like high fructose corn syrup, or additives, Mom would strictly follow along, reading nutrition labels and making sure she did not consume foods that could deter her health. Mom's diet consisted of green leafy vegetables, fresh produce, fish, salad, and fresh fruit. She was diligent, and it showed.

She had the softest skin and very few wrinkles. Folks often commented on her beautiful skin, but she worked hard for it, following a nightly skin routine without fail, and it benefited her, without a doubt.

We could never figure out why her skin was so baby-soft. I've taken care of many elderly folks in care facilities, and never have I ever felt skin as soft or wrinkle-free. Her hair was also, not showing signs of aging, barely graying, at all. Sure, she added color just to get some highlights or lift the richness of her natural strawberry blonde hair, but for a woman in her seventies, almost in her eighties, she barely had any gray. Why am I telling you this, you may wonder? She cared about her health. She cared about what she ate. She cared what the consequences were. No one in the family cared for their health like Mom, no one.

Getting older also had setbacks. Mom soon found out she had osteoarthritis, and her bones were fragile. Now, turning seventy, she took her calcium supplements and drank her milk, in hopes of saving what bone strength she had. Other than the occasional backache, from time to time, or an old injury creeping in, the fragility of her bone health didn't seem to pose a problem yet. On a cold, icy morning, Mom looked through the kitchen window on the frigid day. Fully dressed for the day, she stepped onto the black ice, on the top step to retrieve the daily newspaper.

The ice took her balance from under her, and she was slammed to the ground, leg outstretched, foot wedged against the railing, rotating the ankle. Dad ran quickly to her aid and backed her into the house on her bottom. They quickly realize this is no ordinary injury.

Looking down, they see Mom's foot is no longer in the normal position. It is backward. The ambulance came, and after many X-rays and CT scans, they found that Mom had severed her foot from the leg, and it was only hanging on by tendons. Surgery was necessary immediately to save the foot. I was present when the doctor came in and rotated her foot to the normal position, and I could barely watch. Mom, being Mom, hardly winced, to the doctor's complete surprise. She was a rock. Hours later, Mom emerges from surgery with many plates and screws holding her foot together and a cast. Mom returned home with a full boot, and months of physical therapy followed. She followed her doctor's orders religiously and was determined to get back to herself.

Painful as it was, she forged on. She would come out from therapy in obvious discomfort but also with a tremendous spirit of determination. Soon, her bones healed, and although left weaker than before, we were relieved she had pulled through. Mom would often raise her fist in the air and proclaim, "Yes, I did it," "You did it, Vick," or "Not bad for an old lady." cheering herself on with her amazing spirit and will to live.

Shortly after turning seventy-one, Mom was chatting on the phone with my Aunt and found herself having difficulty talking. Knowing this, she keeps an eye open all day. Mom calls me to voice her concerns, and we diligently watch, hoping it was perhaps a migraine, something she had suffered with for years. The following day, she seemed to have a normal day with no issues, and everything appeared to be okay. I went to work like any other day, and this day, I was interrupted on my break by a phone call from home. I reluctantly answered, heart beating in my chest, to hear my sister's panicked voice. Mom can't talk! The ambulance is on the way. In tears, I rushed out of work and arrived home to the paramedics loading Mom into the ambulance.

I told her I loved her, and she said, "I love you. I'm sorry."

We met her at the hospital and had to wait for the doctor. Her speech returned as we nervously awaited the diagnosis. After CT scans, the doctor arrives, to inform us that it appears to be a TIA, a Trans Ischemic Attack, better known as a mini-stroke. The doctor decides to administer a drug called TPA. This medicine will dissolve the clot, but she will also have to go on blood thinners for the rest of her life. This mini-stroke is often the warning of a more serious stroke to come. We are nervous but hopeful, that is until we look down. There on Mom's blanket was something that caught our eyes. Could it be? Am I seeing what I think I'm seeing? As clear as it can be, there, in all its glory, is a cross about 2 inches long by 1 inch wide. It appears to be rust in color on a white, thick hospital blanket, a perfect cross! Our eyes were wide, and Mom smiled like she wasn't surprised. The kind of smile you smile, when you know you are loved. The doctor returns and sees what we see." Well, it looks like you have someone on your side," he said. Now, we are hopeful. Now we feel God's presence. We are enveloped with a feeling of security. Mom arrived home, and as we were helping her in the house, a monarch butterfly landed on her shoulder, another sign from heaven. She is going to be okay and we are ecstatic. Mom was back home now and prescribed blood thinners. She tested herself regularly. The home blood testing was something she was very proud to have mastered.

Her diet needed to be changed as certain foods can interact with the meds in the blood clotting factors. Cranberry, being one of her favorites, is one of the foods she has to bid farewell to, and she does so, no questions asked. Soon, daily life returns to normal, and things seem to settle down. Once she recovered from these events, she appeared to have the next eight years, seemingly without issue. The Grandchildren were now older, and Matthew graduated from high school. Mom and Dad were enjoying their time together. On my days off, I would take them out for lunch, or spend time at their house. Years pass, and now it's Felicia's time to shine! Yes, she is graduating!

Some things stand out more than others. Usually, these things we remember well. The major milestones, or things that leave an impression on us, good or bad, happy or sad, are the things that stand out. My Mother amazed me. There wasn't much she couldn't do, but there were a few things that stood out, and that graduation gown was one of them.

For some reason, Felicia was the last to get a graduation gown and received it the day before. The gown they gave her was not her size and when I called they said they ran out of other sizes. Here we were the night before graduation with a gown that didn't fit. She was in tears, and I was beyond upset for her. Graduation was a special day, and she worked hard to get here, as did we, and this is what was happening.

Mom was in control. She checked her fabric boxes, and soon Mom said," Let's go to the store to find fabric." We traveled the thirty-minute ride to Massachusetts, as our town no longer carried fabric. Mom browsed the racks. We pulled out things we thought would work, but Mom had a particular quality of material she knew she needed." I've got it," she said, placing the fabric in the shopping cart. We stopped for pizza to celebrate and headed home, as Mom knew she had work to do. Arriving home, Nana wasted no time. She took her machine out, threaded it, and at seventy-five years old, started disassembling the graduation gown. Using her seam ripper, she painstakingly worked on the back seams until the gown was in two pieces. The machine rumbled as she inserted the fabric pieces, measured to create the perfect fit.

Time passed as she sat sewing, determined to make this gown fit for Felicia. Soon, she appeared with the new gown in hand, "Okay, come try it on Fala," as she lovingly called her. Felicia slipped into the white gown Mom was holding and zipped it up! It fit her beautifully, and Felicia was thrilled. Mom clapped with joy, and we hugged her tightly, kissed her, and thanked her over and over. Mom was pleased, and we were beyond grateful for our talented little seamstress. This lady was truly our hero. Beautifully sewn, one couldn't see that the gown had been altered, and Felicia marched across the stage proudly, as we looked on with the biggest smiles and many tears.

As Mom neared the end of her seventies, she was feeling quite well. She kept track of her diet and meds and took her vitals daily with a wrist monitor device that was very accurate. One evening, Mom called me to say she felt a bit odd. She had checked her vitals, and her pulse was very slow. We immediately jumped in the car and went to the house. Mom was sitting on the couch with the device on her lap. Felicia wrapped Nana in her arms to comfort her, and Mom rested her head on Felicia's chest. After some quiet time, we agreed we should check her pulse again. This time, Mom's vitals appeared normal, and we were all relieved, yet cautiously so. We stayed and chatted about going to the Emergency room, but she promised if she felt that way again, she would go, immediately. I reluctantly went home. Shortly after we fell asleep, the phone rang. The phone ringing at 2:00 a.m. was never going to be good news, and my heart sank. It was the paramedic telling me Mom had called 911 and told Dad to get dressed, she was going to the hospital. They decided to take her directly to the hospital 45 minutes away, which specialized in heart procedures. They assured me she was okay, and off they went. After much testing, it was determined that Mom needed a pacemaker.

We arrived at the hospital to find Mom was in good spirits. She was happily chatting with the nurses and was relieved to see us. Mom was nervous about the procedure but knew she needed it. She was so proud that she had decided to call 911 to save her life, and so were we. The surgery was a success, and the cardiologist said the pacemaker was expected to last ten years. Soon, Mom was discharged from the hospital, with new meds and a new suggested routine. Mom followed every rule, exactly, and was now, more determined than ever to keep herself well, although she would joke that the device would outlive her, for sure.

Mom continued to do well. For the most part, aging seemed to be going pretty well, for both, Mom and Dad. The next four years were mostly uneventful. All the grandchildren graduated, and we continued to spend all our spare time with each other and were most grateful to be able to do so. We loved to have Mom and Dad over at our house for dinner dates. Mom would always dress up. She would style her hair, with her makeup applied perfectly, and her jewelry always matched the occasion. She'd arrive with a big hello and always compliment our table setting and dinners.

We would enjoy a wonderful dinner with dessert, and warm tea would follow. Spending time on the porch before sunset made for special memories. It was one of those dinner dates that Mom found herself in a situation of sorts.

One crisp November afternoon, Mom was getting ready for our harvest dinner. Mom stepped back while in the bathroom and caught her leg on a stand, which caused her to lose her balance. She fell to the floor and winced in pain. She knew she had hurt her back but did not want to disappoint us. She arrived at our house, and I immediately could see Mom was uncomfortable. I asked her what was wrong, and she replied, "Oh, it's nothing. I took a little fall in the bathroom and hurt my back. I took some Tylenol, so we'll see." She insisted on staying for dinner and ate, well, but I could see her wince from time to time. I offered to take her to get X-rayed, but she wanted to wait and see.

The next day it was apparent that she needed to be seen by a doctor. So I took her to the Emergency room. X-rays showed that Mom had broken her back, but only time would help it heal.Cortisone shots and prednisone were routine, and Mom was trying to deal with the pain, although she was certainly tired from it. She would say, "I'm not sure how much longer I can stand this pain," this was very unlike Mom. Mom didn't like to be kept down. She loved to be active and kept busy. Her back injury was certainly slowing her down quite a bit. Soon, my sister found a doctor who could inject her back with cortisone directly, and lo and behold it seemed to do the trick! Mom was so happy to be feeling better, and after physical therapy, she was starting to gain strength. I took her to physical therapy weekly for months at our local hospital, and the reward came one day when Mom said, "You know, I think I'm starting to feel better. My back hasn't hurt in a few days now."We were thrilled to know she was in less pain.

What more could we ask for? Soon, Mom was feeling good enough to resume her normal routines, and we were back to our lunches and shopping days. She moved a bit slower now, and more cautiously, but she was back in the land of living, as she would say. The summer of 2017 was a good one. Mom was feeling better, and the good weather always helped. We resumed our dinner dates and spent weekends enjoying my porch on sunny, warm days. Mom always loved a good fudge pop or popsicle, so I always made sure to have them on hand for the special moments spent together. Most summers, we spent warm sunny days in the pool, but this summer Mom wasn't up to it. "Come on, Mom, it's warm. It will be good on your back." "It's okay. I'll get in when I feel up to it." Mom would reply. Mom's back issue played a role in her ability to feel as strong as she had before, and apparently, this left her feeling a bit vulnerable. Mom would often come outside by the pool while we were floating about to ask, "How's the water?" "What's the temp?" You could tell she wanted to come in, but the back injury had taken its toll.

CHAPTER 17

The Last Good Summer

Getting older is never easy, and unfortunately, Mom was not exempt from this natural process. Summer was in full swing now, so we'd visit the clam shack by the beach for fish and chips and clam cakes. Mom loved this time. We'd sit in the car, windows down by the water, while I doled out forks, tartar sauce, and drinks. The smell of vinegar and fish filled the car, and the warm wind rustled our hair slightly, blowing in the warm sunshine onto our laps. This was summer at its best in New England. I purchased a nice foldable support chair for Mom for her back, and we'd bring it along to make it easier on her because, let's face it, the benches are no picnic for older folks, and none of us were getting any younger.

It was Mom's 84th Birthday, and a trip to that clam shack was the choice of celebration, a beautiful late afternoon day made for good conversation, smiles, laughter, and good food. She looked amazing as always and complimented me on the beautiful cake. "Did you make this, Jen?" "It's so beautiful." Gifts followed, and, as always, she was delighted with her day, and we were happy to celebrate it with her. She'd say, "Eighty-four, who would've ever believed it." She'd put her fist in the air and say, "Yes, I'm still here! God willing, my poor mother was only fifty- two, and here I am eighty- four. Next year, I'll be eighty-five. Can you imagine?"In the evening, our phone calls always included Mom thanking us for a wonderful day. She would say, "Aren't we fortunate to have each other on this beautiful day." She'd often sit outside and say, "What a day, the sun is shining, the birds are singing, who could ask for more," or "What a beautiful day for a wedding." She constantly found beauty in what others called ordinary. I was always amazed by her positivity. I'm so happy that so many of our days were spent together. I would take them for rides from one part of the island to the other, Mom saying," Well Jen, that was a wonderful day. We had lunch and a beautiful ride, and you spoiled me with beautiful things.

I am one fortunate lady" Then she'd make a cup of "nice warm tea" as she called it, and have a cookie. Summer ended, and fall blew in. On September 5th, we celebrated Mom and Dad's sixty-fourth wedding anniversary. We had family, dinner, and cake. What a milestone! Sixty-four years as husband and wife. They were always so proud of their long marriage.

One afternoon, Mom surprised me by telling me she had ordered a new bathing suit for next year. I was excited to hear this as it meant she was feeling better and was looking forward to enjoying the water next summer! This was exciting, and when it arrived, she tried it on by modeling it for us. "So what do you think?" "Should I've gotten a bigger size? "Does it show my stomach?" What tummy, Mom?" I asked, "Oh, I have one." She'd reply, "I feel it, it feels different." " I can't see anything Mom. It looks great," I answered. (This is one of those times that makes me think). A dark blue, all-in-one, with a sweet little ruffled skirt, it was a perfect suit and looked adorable on her. Mom put her new suit in a tote bag, with a towel, in hopes of using it next summer.

November and December found us in the usual routine, shopping for Christmas.

I worked the closing shift at a retail establishment as closing manager. So when I got home around 10, I would stop over to Mom to say hello, and she would always ask how my day was. She would often be on the phone with my Aunt and would say, "Oh, Jen's home, I'll go," I would say, 'No, no, Mom, go ahead and chat, and I'll talk to you after I get settled" I'd reach down and kiss her, she'd kiss me, and she would blow me a kiss, as I walked away. When I got home, we would sometimes chat for hours.

Christmas was coming quickly, and as our family was getting older, we were out of ideas. I worked in a store with beautiful gifts, so I was happy to bring home gifts to check off on Mom's shopping list. She was so pleased and would immediately wrap them beautifully, with hopes for a memorable Christmas. Decorating for Christmas was so special for Mom. She would set up all the Christmas carolers on the top of the piano, each representing a family member. She used to have a large 7-foot Victorian decorated tree, but as she got older, she went to a small tabletop tree. The small tree had beautiful ornaments, and I purchased smaller, lighter ornaments to fill it in. The manger Dad built years ago sat beside the tree. The house felt festive, and we were all looking forward to another wonderful Christmas together.

Mom had started to say the rosary a lot more lately. She would watch mass in the morning and say the rosary at night, but amazingly enough, she had decided to teach herself how to pray the rosary in three languages, Spanish, French, and Italian. She was thrilled to have mastered this, and when we arrived, she would excitedly show us how she could speak the rosary in those languages. She was beyond delighted to serve the Lord and to do so in another language. Mom loved education and keeping her mind busy. She believed if you kept your mind active, you could stay young and keep your brain healthy. So, at age 84, she taught herself the rosary in three languages and didn't stop there. She wanted to learn to play the guitar, so my brother bought her a new guitar and a book. She'd sit for hours with her guitar and book, and because she knew how to read music, she learned rather quickly. With my brother's help, she was making progress and was so pleased when she could play a song to sing along with. We videotaped her as she was so proud. What an incredible Mother we have. We were so proud of her.

Christmas was blessed. We celebrated at my house, and although Mom was tired, we were happy to have dinner, exchange gifts, and spend time celebrating. A large turkey was the centerpiece on the table, with mashed potatoes, corn, and sweet potatoes. Hot dinner rolls sprinkled with cinnamon, pearl onions, and applesauce filled the decorative bowls. After dinner, desserts filled the table. Pumpkin pie, apple pie, vanilla ice cream, and maple cookies were the perfect endings to a wonderful celebration. With tummies full, they would all rest up in the living room while Felicia and I did the dishes. Mom would always offer help, and I always declined.

Once the kitchen was tidy, it was time to exchange our gifts. One of the very special gifts Mom gave me was a gold bracelet with the entire Our Father prayer etched on a gold disc. It was so beautiful and a gift of faith. We finished the evening unwrapping presents and enjoying each other's company. How very fortunate we were to have another blessed Christmas. Soon, New Year's was here, and as always, we called each other to say Happy New Year! at midnight and say I love you We were hoping 2018 was going to be another year of blessings, another year of family, love, and support. We were hoping … anyway.

CHAPTER 18

Expect the Unexpected

Dad's 85th Birthday. We celebrated as a family at a local Chinese buffet. The whole family came. We had cake and presents and shared stories. Mom enjoyed it, as she loved it when her entire family was together. We took pictures and many of them. I'm so glad we did. It was a great night, but unbeknownst to us, it would be the last of its kind. It's all she ever wanted, family and she worked hard to achieve it. She wanted all her children to get along and all the grandkids to love each other.

She loved cookouts with everyone there. She would bring out all her matching plastic plates and the ice bucket full of ice cubes she had made the night before. Dad would make his famous potato salad, and Mom baked beans with brown sugar. One by one, we'd arrive with our dishes of macaroni salad and taco salad, corn on the cob, chips, watermelon, and Mom's much-loved, chocolate-covered brownies.

Hot dogs were Mom's favorite, and hamburgers were available too, a favorite for sure. Mom was always so happy at family cookouts, sweet memories that will last a lifetime. When we finished eating and helping with cleaning up, the kids would all get in the pool for hours of fun. My brother's boys especially enjoyed the pool, as they lived over an hour away, and we didn't see them often. Having everyone on these occasions made the day extra special for Mom, and she would always be smiling. Dessert time would mean everyone out of the pool, and while singing Happy Birthday, you could always hear Mom harmonizing while yelling speech, speech! Loud clapping and laughter filled the backyard. Special times together are memories no one can take away, and I'm so glad we were so fortunate to experience that precious time.

One never knows when to expect the unexpected. We can't. We wake up expecting a "normal day." You go about your usual, not realizing for most of that time, the shoe can fall at any moment. Have you ever been in a large crowd and thought, wow, look, here we all are. Everyone's heart is beating, and their brains are functioning. That in itself is miraculous. To have thirty thousand people in a stadium or concert, and no one is experiencing medical trauma, is truly, amazing.

We are blind to what may be happening on the inside, and one never knows when something will go wrong. Ticking time bombs, some may say. God willing, others will voice after making plans. Fragile, we are. One should always expect the unexpected.

The day started like most of us, except Dad was having a few teeth extracted. February 1st is an easy date to remember, but a day I'd much rather forget. I was working the night shift from 3 to 10 that day, so I told Dad I'd pick him up to bring him to the dentist. I arrived, and Mom sent us off with good luck wishes and smiles. Within the hour, we returned home. Dad had a mouthful of gauze, and Mom was ready to care for him. I gave her the instructions and headed to the pharmacy to pick up the pain meds. I got the meds, dropped them off to him, and headed home. When I arrived home, I took out the ingredients to make bread pudding. This delicious dish was Mom's recipe, of course, and we devoured it when she made it.

I had decided that since he'd be on a soft diet for a few days, I would quadruple the recipe, so I got out my large roasting pan. Pouring in the hot milk with sweet sugar and vanilla, I was eager to surprise him. There would be plenty for Mom to enjoy as well. I put my very heavy, lovingly prepared mix into the oven and started getting ready for work. The timer went off. I removed the finished delicacy from the hot oven and onto the counter to cool. Soon, it was time to go, and I wrapped the pan in foil for the ride. Still warm, the sweet smell of cinnamon and nutmeg made my nostrils flare and taste buds flow.

I arrived at Mom and Dad's with the hot pan. Mom would ooh and aah as usual and commented on the very large quantity. "Look at the size of this, Jen!" "This is going to be delicious." I made room in the fridge for the large pan, but not before scooping out large tablespoons of soft, fluffy cinnamon custard goodness into small glass bowls. I delivered one bowl to Dad, who was in the living room recliner, and he seemed eager to try it. Mom sat at the kitchen table, tasting her portion, eyes closed, savoring the sweetness in her mouth." This is delicious, Jen, but I'll save mine for dessert."

I was pleased and kissed them goodbye to head off to work. Work was an average night. I rearranged the jewelry counter with my coworker, and we were satisfied with the results. It was a bitter, bitter evening when we left the store that night. We stood shivering in the dark lot, chatting a bit. The cold forced us into our cars, and I noticed the time. "Dang! 10:15 p.m., it's so late. I shouldn't have chatted". I don't know why I felt that way, but I specifically remember, feeling the need to get home.

I arrived at Mom and Dad's to pick up my daughter, who was there visiting. When I arrived at their house, I was met at the door by my Father. "Your Mother fell in the kitchen. She's sore, but please check her out." I went into the living room to find my daughter comforting Mom. Mom was very uncomfortable and not herself. I immediately said we had to go to the hospital. Mom wasn't too keen on the idea, as none of us would be, but she knew she needed to go and didn't have a choice, so she didn't argue. I called the ambulance, and they came right away. I followed the ambulance to the hospital, five minutes away, leaving Dad and my daughter home.

 In the Emergency room, they ran tests, CAT scans, X-rays, and blood work, and after seven hours, admitted her for observation.

I left the hospital at 6:00 a.m. and kissed her, telling her I'd be back. I could hear her telling the nurse I was her baby and that I was so good to her. Beautiful Mom, even in pain, still bragging about me. I didn't deserve that beautiful woman, but I knew, without a doubt, I was beyond blessed.

I went home, showered, and picked up Dad to return to the hospital. By now, my brother and sister had arrived, and we headed up to her room. Mom was receiving blood transfusions, and we found she was severely anemic. She had been tired, and her hair was thinning, but she had an upcoming appointment in just days.

The fall happened while she was getting up to warm up some carrots in the microwave. She later said she had heard a high-pitched beeping and then passed out, hitting her body on the stove and microwave cart. She hit her knees, elbows, and forehead on the hard, white, ceramic-tiled kitchen floor. Good God Almighty. It was dreadful! My poor, wonderful mother was eighty-four years old and had a horrific fall that changed her life forever, and we would all never be the same.

CHAPTER 19

A Bad Dream

Soon after they admitted Mom, we found our way to her room. She was badly bruised, and her back was in terrible pain. She was not feeling well and appeared quite fragile. She was quiet and seemed vague. That night we sang," Let There Be Peace on Earth" to her, and she sang along with my brother and me. This time together reduced my brother to tears, and he excused himself to the bathroom for a full-blown cry. Never, had we seen our mother so weak and battered, and yet, this poor, poor darling was singing her favorite song. It's a sad but dear memory for me, as it made her happy but hurt us to see her poor physical state. After receiving many blood transfusions, Mom began to hallucinate and yell out loud. We were terrified. They moved her to the Intensive Care Unit, to monitor her and ran more tests to see if anything else was manifesting after this terrible fall. In the Intensive care unit, she seemed as though she was starting to get better. She chatted while we visited. She talked with me about losing her mother and how sad it was.

She spoke about the fact that losing her Mom was a pain like no other and that she was glad she had only had to go through that once. Hearing this meant that the pain was far greater than she had ever let on, and she knew what we would have to experience, and this scared the daylights out of me. Mom also said that she wasn't sure she'd make it out of this one. Did she know? I remember that so well, and the feeling I had when she said it. It took my breath away. I couldn't even fathom it, not even for a second.

Mom spent quite some time in the Intensive Care Unit, and we were hopeful that she was going to make a full recovery. We put pictures of the family on her tray table and brought rosaries in for her, as she loved to hold them and found immense comfort with them. Flowers, balloons, and teddy bears also filled the room. All these things seemed to help tremendously, and she seemed to be coming around, getting back to herself. The Intensive Care Unit was a place of twists and turns, and often they were sudden. Suddenly, Mom started to fade and wasn't responding. The Doctor ordered more tests, but the results were inconclusive. She went on like this for some time.

One morning, the phone rang. I answered nervously, only to hear, "Hi darling," "Oh my God!" Well, look who's up!" I replied. I cried happy tears and drove there as fast as I could. I was greeted by Mom waving to me with her beautiful smile. "Hi, Jen," I was reduced to tears. We hugged and spent the day visiting, learning they managed to get her heart back in proper rhythm. The cardiology team believed the erratic heart rate may have contributed to the health issues and that the **virus** she had so many years ago had affected her heart to a greater extent. We were shocked to hear this, and the news left us shaking our heads in disbelief.

Soon after close monitoring and medication changes, Mom was moved to a room with close monitoring, out of the Intensive Care Unit, and we took this as great news! We were on cloud nine for sure. We all spent the days beside her visiting, bringing in things from home, her glasses, magazines, and the bread pudding she requested. She hadn't forgotten! That excitement didn't last long, and soon, they transferred Mom back to the Intensive Care Unit for more monitoring. We took pictures on good days and bad. We had made a get-well sign and hung it in her room.

One day, while she lay quietly and mainly unresponsive, she opened her eyes and commented that she admired the sign hanging on the wall, however, it needed a comma between that word and another. She smiled that smile she gave us when she knew she was right, and we all laughed with her for being the grammar police she'd always been. Now that's my Mom! Maybe she was going to get better!

Soon, Mom started having ICU delirium from her lengthy stay. The doctor informed us that this delirium is a condition that happens to adults, usually over fifty, when they are in the Intensive Care Unit for long periods. Having no windows, no time, no daylight, no night, the beeping noises, and being tied to machines all take a toll on the mind. You lose track of time and space, like a prisoner of war. It was frightening to see this, so we brought in a picture of a sun and a moon. We put it up in a frame, on a stand, and it would say good morning, the sun is shining, and Good evening, the moon is out. We brought in a CD player for music, and soon, Mom seemed to come around. She was transferred to a regular room and seemed to be heading in the right direction.

One evening, Mom had a new roommate, and to our surprise, her boyfriend was in bed with her after hours. I immediately notified the nurse that I wasn't okay with a man in my Mother's room. The nurse in charge asked the man to leave, and I requested that Mom be assigned a different room. It was late, so I kissed Mom goodbye and felt confident the room change would follow.

The next day, Mom was in a private room, much to my delight. I was going through her things when I noticed that the two stuffed toys I had brought her were missing. I let the nurse know things were missing, and they told me the roommate must have taken them. Mom hadn't been moved to the new room until morning. I was not happy and would find out that the roommate was a homeless, troubled woman who had helped herself to Mom's things. I was furious and worried that perhaps this woman could have hurt Mom, but that thought was too hard to bear, and there was no evidence, of such. She seemed happy and unaffected, now safely in her new room.

Visits continued, and one evening, Mom asked me to stay the night. The nurse brought me some pillows and a blanket, and I slept in the lounge chair beside her bed.

To our surprise, the following day, they said it was time to go home!! Wow, wow, wow! What a day! We were just ecstatic! I held my breath, and we brought her home. I pulled up on the lawn close to the front stairs while the family got on either side to help her up the stairs and into the house as she was still in terrible pain with her back. We got her seated and celebrated her being home. Thank you, Jesus! This day was a day to celebrate! The family arrived to see the momentous occasion. Matthew shared the news that he was expecting to be a father, and Mom and Dad, great-grandparents. Overall, it was a happy day, and she was home!

Mom being back home was exciting but scary as well, as her pain level was high, and she still seemed a bit fragile. Every day, I would arrive early in the morning to help, bathe, and dress her, then get her from the bed to her chair in the living room. Once she was settled, Dad would deliver breakfast on the tray, and we would watch the morning show. While she was resting, I'd leave Dad to stay with her and go home to get ready for work. On my way to work, I'd drop Felicia off to care for my Mother and help Dad in the evening.

Once my shift ended, I'd go over to my parents' home and get Mom ready for bed. Sometimes, Felicia would surprise me and do it for me, a nice treat after my long day. We had a sweet little routine. I'd help her up, and we'd dance to the bed in small, stepped circles to the song, " I could have danced all night, I could have danced all night," We'd laugh because, soon, we found we weren't getting too far along in the song, by the time we made it to the bed. This meant she was getting faster, and the transfer was going smoother. Some evenings, she asked me to stay a while longer, and I'd lay beside her on the bed. We'd talk about plans on what to do next, and then I'd leave around 1:30 a.m. to go home to sleep and return in the morning.

This schedule continued for the time she was home. Occasionally, my brother and sister would come over and bring dinner, or stay the weekend, to give me some time off. One particular day will remain in my memory forever. Snug in her new pink, plush pajamas, we lay side-by-side on the bed, arms around each other. Mom looked at me and said, "My baby, you're so cute." I laughed because I didn't think I was cute, but she did and said, "You were always so cute," "Julie was a pretty baby, Ken, handsome, but you were always cute."

Then she said, "What would I do without you?" I answered, "What would I do without you?" "I'm afraid you'll have to find out. This time is different, it feels different," she said. "Oh, don't say that. I'll die." I replied. "No, you won't. I raised you better than that." "You have to be strong for your daughter. It won't be easy, but it's part of life," she replied. I swallowed hard, trying not to cry, hoping the giant lump in my throat would go away. I kissed her and hugged her, taking her all in, as though it was our last hug.

I adored this woman and didn't want to let her go. I promised her that day we'd find out what was wrong with her back, so I made calls the next day. I brought her to the orthopedic doctor. It was so difficult to get her out of the house. The amount of pain she was experiencing limited her mobility, but we did it. Bringing along a wheelchair I purchased for her was very helpful in getting her in and out of medical appointments. X-rays were painful, and getting up on the hard table, and positioning her was excruciating. I comforted her and assisted. The doctor read the X-rays and returned to the exam room with the results. Nothing was wrong, just bruising, "After all, she is eighty-four," they would say.

I would make another appointment with another doctor at the hospital. She would endure more X-rays and more tests. These appointments were very painful for Mom, but I promised we'd find out what was wrong.

One last appointment remained, and my sister took her this time to the spine specialist at the hospital. The doctor was very kind. He examined Mom and ordered X-rays. The next day, I was at work when I took the call from the doctor himself, and I'll never forget his words, "Jennifer, this is Doctor Kyle. I saw your Mother yesterday." " I have some bad news. Your Mother's back is fractured in 3 places. These fractures are the reason for her extreme pain." Dear God! Are you serious? She knew it! She did, and they all said she was okay. I was furious with the other doctors, who tossed it up to the fragility of an elderly lady! Every one of those doctors missed the findings in the X-rays and exams! Unacceptable! Although, now we had an answer, and maybe with a solution, she could recover and be without pain. Mom was relieved to know the pain wasn't in her head, but she was also scared of how we would proceed.

The pain was only increasing now, and she was feeling very different. A bladder infection set her back, but the meds did the trick, and soon she was back to herself. Mom seemed well, doing puzzles, talking on the phone, and discussing options for her recovery. During this time, we were hoping that since she seemed to be more like herself, her back was our last hurdle. After much thought and consideration, a plan was in place for her to have surgery to cement her broken back. If we hadn't chosen this option, it would have taken six months or more to heal, and the pain was getting the best of her.

Suddenly, Mom started to hallucinate, and her 02 would drop. She was hospitalized in April, leaving the house for what we now know was the last time. Once Mom was in the local hospital, we soon learned that her iron was very low again. The anemia was the reason for her changes. Mom was given more blood transfusions, and it was recommended that she be placed in the intensive care unit for close monitoring. Soon, she was well enough for surgery, and I had to consent. I'll never forget leaning over her in the pre-surgical room. We were still unsure if this surgery was the right decision.

Mom wearily looked up at me and spoke in a soft voice of question. "I don't know, what do you think? Should I do it?" I answered nervously, my heart, in my stomach, "I don't know, Mom. The doctor said, "It's the best way to heal your back, if not, it will take six months to recover." "Well, I guess we should do it then, huh?" Mom asked. Rubbing her hand, I replied, "I guess so, Mom." I signed the consent form, head spinning, kissed her, and prayed like I had never prayed before, and off she went.

Recovery wasn't going smoothly, as she wasn't experiencing much pain relief. Soon, Mom drifted into a state of unresponsiveness. I was desperate for answers and started my intense research into the mystery of my Mom's illness. Should I have signed those damn consent forms? Did the cement leak? That was one of the risks. What the hell was happening? These thoughts in my head were enough to kill me. Oh God, please! In the weeks that followed, she continued to go downhill. They ran test after test until the doctor in charge of her care came in to speak with us. "I think your Mother may be dying. She is not eating or responding, and if she were my Mother, I'd take her somewhere else.

Our family agreed we needed to make that move, and the doctor started making phone calls to Rhode Island Hospital Trauma Center or Boston General. Later that day, the doctor informed us it would be Rhode Island Hospital. They had a room.

CHAPTER 20

Devastation

Mom had been in Rhode Island Hospital for about a week now. I could not visit her, because I had a terrible cough and cold, and frankly, I should have been hospitalized. I wouldn't dare bring my sickness to my Mother, who was already fighting for her life. One evening, while Dad and Julie were visiting with Mom, she was awake and talking. They fed her small amounts of dinner and noticed her left arm was quite swollen. Julie, being a nurse, brought this to the attention of the doctor, who assured her that these things happen sometimes and that they were watching her. Julie sent me the picture, which I found concerning. I asked Julie what they were doing about her arm and why it was so swollen, and she said the doctor said it was being observed and called it a flash flood effect. I, however, was not convinced, but that's nothing new. By this time, it would've taken an act of God to convince me that the medical care my Mother was receiving was adequate.

They visited until quite late that evening, 10:30 p.m., and filled me in on the evening on their way home. I called the floor that evening at approximately 11:30 p.m. and spoke to the nurse caring for my Mother. I asked why my Mother was not on the floor that was monitoring her more closely, and she responded that this was the only room available and, presently, Mom did not require intensive care. I brought all my concerns to this nurse and reiterated my fear of her not being closely monitored. She assured me that she was in and out of the room and that they would keep a close eye on her.

Less than a half-hour after I spoke to the nurse, Mom was found in respiratory arrest. A code blue was announced throughout the hospital, and they all ran. One of the nurses who had answered that code told me her heart never stopped, but it was intense, leading to her falling deep into a comatose state. That night, the doctors intubated my Mother, and the start of the long, dark journey was ahead of us. This scenario is what plays in my head continuously. How long was she in distress?

Did she know? Did she cry out? Panic? These questions can take my breath and stop my heart. Dear

God, oh dear God. The phone calls traumatized me, and I'm forever terrified by the sound of my phone ringing late hours to this day. The phone rang at 12:38 p.m., and I was startled awake.

I answered groggily, heart pounding. It was the doctor, calling to tell me that Mom was having seizure-like movements, and was in respiratory arrest." Hurry, he said, "It's bad." I couldn't drive at night, as I have night-vision issues. I didn't know how to get there, so I froze. I called my sister and my brother, and they drove up immediately. I felt helpless waiting by the phone, scared to death, crying with all my heart, praying with all my might. I didn't call Dad, I didn't want to wake him, scare him, and then put him at risk of a medical emergency. At 85 you tread lightly around them.

My sister and brother arrived to see Mom hooked up to life support, tubes all over her body. They sent a picture to me, and I sobbed. My beautiful, beautiful Mother suffered a near-fatal medical trauma. My poor, poor girl. In the morning, I went to Dad's to tell him that Mom had a medical incident and she was not well.

My brother came back to drive us up. I'll never forget that horrible moment seeing her hooked up to all those machines, keeping her alive. Seeing your loved one on life support is shocking and takes the very breath out of you. Her eyes were partially open, and we tried to see if she could see us, but she couldn't. I am here to tell you that there is nothing worse in life than seeing your loved one lifeless, helpless, and so unreachable. This tragedy was the beginning of the end. Life as we knew it was over.

May came and went in silence, and our shattered hearts were heavy. My brother took a leave of absence, and I left my job. We all sat at her bedside from morning till night. One evening, while visiting, Julie was escorted to a small room down the hallway in the Intensive care unit, where an intern told her Mom had Mad cow disease and would die. Dad lost it upon hearing this and was inconsolable. Crying, howling," Oh God no, oh God no, I want my wife, I want my wife, oh darlin' no!" It was horrible. It will haunt me forever, along with all the traumatic images and thoughts. We arrived at the hospital the next day in tears over the new, unthinkable, unheard-of diagnosis. How, in God's name, would she have contracted such a disease? How? Standing by her bed, caressing her hands, we were in tears at the thought of this horrible disease ravishing her body.

The head nurse, who happened to be the gentleman who had answered the code blue on Mom, entered the room. "Why the tears today?" He asked. We told him the intern had said Mom had Mad cow disease, and he immediately ran off and quickly returned with the doctor. The doctor led us down the hallway to a small room. The small room scared us to death, and we did not know what to expect. The doctor put his hand on Dad's knee and started to speak. "I understand my intern told you your wife has Mad cow disease. I want you to know that this is not the case. She does NOT have Mad cow disease, and I apologize for this." Dad sobbed and sobbed. My heart broke for him, yet we rejoiced in the new, welcomed good news. Thank God, but poor Dad was never the same after that day. I honestly believe that the trauma took a piece of his heart.

Trauma will do that, it really will. Eventually, Mom was moved to a respiratory Intensive Care Unit, where she remained for four months. According to the specialist, this is the unit where they missed her lung abscess. Day after day, we sat by Mom's bedside with hopeful hearts. After one month in the Intensive care unit, they removed the ventilation and replaced it with a tracheostomy. This is a tube that is surgically placed in the airway. She looked better and more peaceful, but we knew that the tracheostomy meant she was in serious condition. While we kept vigil by Mom's bedside we would watch as the trauma helicopter landed outside Mom's window. Thump, thump, thump, the copter came to a stop on the landing pad to unload a critical care patient. Feeling their pain, our silent prayers went up to God through our view from our window. Code blue, Code blue, bellowed throughout the corridors, more times than we'd like to hear, and again, our hearts sank for the families and patients. We couldn't help but take a deep breath, knowing how close we were to being that family again. Occasionally, a box with a sheet over it on a gurney would pass by our room with someone who had passed on, ending their story. Tearful family members walked behind, heads bowed. I hated it for them and felt very vulnerable.

Beep, beep, beep, swish, swish, swish, went the machines keeping Mom alive. The alarms sounded warnings when she was not handling it well, making our hearts jump out of our chests!

Panicked by the alarms, we would immediately rise from our chairs and run to the door, where we would be met immediately by a nurse rushing in to answer the alarms. Nurses, doctors, in and out. Solemn faces with news we didn't want to hear, questions we didn't want to answer.

One particular doctor tending to her often, had no personality. He'd come in and shake his head at us as if we were making her suffer. He always used her age against her and could offer no answers. He missed the lung abscess, and oh, how I wish I knew that then! He and I did not hit it off at all. I'd bring in my research, and he'd raise his eyebrows and roll his eyes, but when questioned, he'd have no answers and no educated advice. He was cold and bored with his job. An unsympathetic robot and I let him know it. He stormed off, ripping his gloves off, as I once again put him in a position where he was blank with answers.

I demanded to see a more seasoned doctor. This doctor was much older and had a warm bedside manner. He offered advice with a kind heart and entertained my medical research respectfully and as a team. From here on, I referred to this doctor with much more confidence.

It's a shame that there are doctors, who have become emotionally unattached to the care of others. Every patient is unique and deserves to be cared for with hope and respect.

Sometimes, heavenly signs are hard to deny. One day, as Mom lay fighting for her life, a new nurse entered the room. She was dark-skinned and had a heavy accent. Looking peaceful and in no hurry, she walked over to Mom and said, "Victoria, wake up, wake up, your family needs you." Dad and I exchanged glances, confused as to why this new nurse, whom we had never met in the four months of being there, had thought she could wake Mom. As delicately as I could, I explained that Mom was in a coma, "No, she is just sleeping!" she replied with a strong, confident, but kind voice. The new nurse walked over to the bedside and proceeded to test Mom's vital signs, which came back with concern. Worried, Dad and I stand and approach Mom's bed to get a better look and be present with our concerns.

This new nurse just smiled and said, "That's ok, you'll see, I'll take them again," She pressed the button on the machine again, and I kid you not, these vitals were textbook vitals. The new nurse replied, "See… Perfect" Yes, they were… perfect! Hmmm, this got me thinking, and Dad gave me a look of surprise with some expression of confusion. Then, without pause, she asked," Do you believe?" to which I replied, "Oh yes, very much, it's all we have," she pointed up to the ceiling and then, staring intently at us, with a deep, commanding voice, she spoke, "YOU MUST BELIEVE!" He is the ALPHA AND THE OMEGA!!!" To say we were dumbstruck was an understatement, as she left me speechless. Dad and I, both wide-eyed and mesmerized, stood in shock. The new nurse walked silently to the computer as we said goodbye to Mom and covered her with kisses. As we were ready to leave, I asked the nurse her name. She replied, "My name is Hope, Have a beautiful life", and to my Father, she replied, "Bye-bye, Poppy."

We walked in silence to the elevator. While we waited for the elevator to reach our floor, Dad looked at me and whispered, "Was that an angel?" Still shocked, and in deep thought, over what just transpired, I shakily replied," I think so, I really do."

The following day, after telling the family about our surreal experience, our regular nurse entered the room. We caught up with small talk, and then she asked who the nurse was on duty yesterday. I told her it was Hope. She replied that she didn't know of a nurse named Hope and that there was no such nurse named Hope. "I'll be right back," She said," I want to see if she was a float from another floor." She returned to the room and said," The charge nurse said there was no one named Hope. There were no floats on this floor during that time, none at all." I told her our story. She was shocked and replied with wide-open eyes. "I think you had a visitor." A visitor from heaven? Could it be? I thought.

No one had an explanation for it, and we were dumbfounded and left wondering what it meant. Perhaps comfort, or an angel, bringing us a reason to keep believing, a messenger of God's strength and hope. A second encounter happened near the end of Mom's journey. My daughter and I were standing in the hallway outside of Mom's hospital room. My daughter had just seen my Mom and was visibly upset at Nana's condition. I was trying to comfort her when this gentleman appeared with a clipboard. He entered the supply closet momentarily, exited with a smile, and walked directly over to us

" Hi," he said, "Can I help you?" I explained that Mom was still with us but very close to ending her journey. He put his finger up in the air and proclaimed, " I can't make miracles, but I can pray." He gathered us in prayer, hands on our shoulders. We gratefully thanked him, and he told us his name. He asked us our names separately, offering blessings to us. He disappeared down the hallway, walking happily. Felicia and I stood in awe of what had just happened. It was a feeling of complete intervention, and we both felt it deeply. Felicia asked, " Was that an angel?" "I think so," I whispered, "but he said he was from administration," "No, Mom," she said, "his tag said consultant.".......God's consultant? An angel in disguise? to bring us peace and comfort? There was no one by his name listed in the hospital. So, you see, we were never alone. God comforted us in his way. He was there all along, all along. The time had come when the doctors felt it was necessary to give us an alternative. The alternative came from the original doctor I asked to step aside due to his lack of empathy. This cold-hearted caregiver, who vowed to "Do no harm," was suggesting that we stop feeding Mom and let her die. Really? She had a fully functioning brain. CT scan after CT scan showed a fully functioning brain, and her vitals were all good. She responded to pain, and in her alert moments, that one day in the hospital, when she had woken, she could follow commands like open your mouth, track movements, smile, and even mouth words. How in the world, would they expect us to stop feeding her, and watch her die, when she was still very present in so many ways? Well, call me selfish, but I wasn't going to be the one to be responsible for my mother's death. God help us. Soon, August was upon us, and it was time to move Mom, to the rehab center in hopes of a recovery, of sorts, if possible.

CHAPTER 21

Research

Night after night, I didn't sleep. I researched every disorder and deficiency one could imagine. My family jokingly called me Google M.D. Let me say this. I believe with all my heart that my findings helped, if not a lot, a little, and something is worth celebrating when there's nothing. "Nothing, nothing wrong, can't find anything." That's what the doctors told us. "It's a mystery," so they chalked it up to dementia, even though her brain showed no signs. Early on in this journey, when Mom stopped being conscious for the first time in the local hospital, doctors would yell her name, press on her chest with their knuckles, tickle her, and scrape the bottoms of her feet to get her to respond. Numerous CTs and spinal taps and still no answers, perhaps dementia, they said. I would question sharply, "Dementia?" She was learning three languages one month ago, organizing the guest room, making storage totes to give to charity, and learning to play the guitar.

She did not have dementia. One afternoon, much
earlier in this journey, the doctor had come in, to
examine Mom. He started the usual, checking reflexes
and yelling, "What's your name?!" Suddenly, to
everyone's surprise, with eyes closed, Mom spoke
clearly and firmly, stating," My name is Victoria, I am
eighty-four years old, I live in Rhode Island, and I can
hear you and understand." To say we were shocked was
an understatement! What a day! The doctors were left
speechless, and we were smiling ear to ear, clapping for
Mom, letting her know how thrilled we were. So, I
would continue to research, night after night, until the
sun came up.

I did not sleep. I learned medical terms that I'd
never heard before. I studied chemical formulas and
diseases so rare even seasoned doctors had no answers.
Every conceivable possibility I explored. I was
determined to bring my mother back at all costs. I'd fill
my legal pad with findings and alternative treatments.
I'd screenshot, save, download, and deliver my research
findings to the head doctors. Most doctors would listen,
and some would not, but I was relentless. One day, the
hospital called a meeting.

We established a date that would work, and I started more of my studies. On the day of the meeting, I entered the conference room with my sister to a team of more than ten doctors. They introduced themselves and what their role was in caring for my mother. We introduced ourselves, and they proceeded to ask us if we had any questions. Questions? That's all I had, and many of them. I opened my yellow legal pad to the first page, pen in hand, and started my quest for answers. Doctors didn't intimidate me, as I had been used to fighting for the answers when my daughter was so ill. I was ready for them. I asked question after question. Some of my questions had them perplexed, unable to answer. To my dismay, they asked me how I was so knowledgeable. They asked if I was a doctor, and when I replied no, one of the Neurologists suggested I should be. I replied, "My knowledge today only comes from the dedication I have to save my mother," "Without loving her and wanting to save her and find an answer to this mystery so badly, I would not hold this knowledge I present to you today." I continued with my research findings and many questions, jotting down their answers.

The meeting lasted about an hour or so, and I felt I had accomplished a lot, as the Doctors had agreed to try some of the medications I had found proven to help in circumstances like Moms. Per my request, additional testing would be performed, and in leaving that meeting, I had some hope.

I will tell you that those days turned into weeks, then months. The worst ten months of our lives. Because when your loved one lies dying, you fight like hell, like you never have before. I wouldn't settle, even if I couldn't save her, I almost died trying, and I was okay with that. But I was ultimately shown, that even in all of your fight, and all of your sheer determination, with all of my ignorance, and the doctor's ignorance of this undiagnosable illness, that life showed its ugliness, its unforgiving, heart-stealing reality, and, I was defeated, but, not before, many, many, small victories, after all, her name is Victoria.

CHAPTER 22

Small but Huge Victories

Victories, Big events, small events, and those that make us clap, rejoice, cheer, jump up and down, cry, and laugh. Emotions are what victories consist of. They come from wishing, hard work, luck, justice, or everyday tasks we all take for granted. It's funny how things we do with little effort become the dreams we wish to achieve when we can't. We like to think we're invincible, strong, and protected as if we have control.

The one thing I've learned through this journey is that we have very little control over anything. The small amount that we do have can result in small, but huge victories. My Mother always seemed to be smiling or laughing. Always pleasant and positive. So, in return, you get what you give if you're lucky, and if luck isn't on luck isn't on your side, well, love could be and in this case, love was the push behind every victory, big and small.

Mom was loved, so very, very loved, and deservedly so. She gave nothing but love, and her family thrived on it. Mom always jumped in with one hundred percent hope and determination in any situation that needed her. Whether it be sick neighbors in need, children, grandchildren, or her husband, she was always behind them, pushing for their victories. She would have it no other way. So, when one of your loved ones is critically ill, as in my Mother's situation, every little something is something big, and we would celebrate those moments as if she were walking on water. We cherished them like gifts from God. I knew my mother like the back of my hand, as she would say, and while she was sleeping, I grew to know her like a mother knows her child. I cared for her, groomed her, sang to her, exercised her body, and knew every mark and freckle.

Our roles seemed as though they had changed, but I knew she was still my mother, and I was still her child, and I was going to do anything I could to bring her back. In July, while still in the trauma hospital, Mom surprised us when we arrived. She was awake!!! To say we were ecstatic doesn't come close! She looked bewildered at all the excitement, and we did our best to gently explain.

We took pictures and were like giddy children, all up close, kissing her and trying to get responses. Amazingly, she smiled, and I swear I felt reborn. The joy in seeing her smile was so immense. She looked so good, and we were all so hopeful. Waking up isn't like you see in the movies. It doesn't happen like that. It's a much harsher reality. Our joy, however, was short-lived. Mom would drift back into her deep slumber the next day.

Towards the end of August, the hospital informed us it was time to move Mom into a facility. I was terrified. I had always reassured Mom that I would never put her in a facility, but having the tracheostomy and needing to be suctioned and monitored, we knew, for now, we were over our heads. Her Afib would sometimes present itself randomly, making it difficult to keep her heart stable.

I'm not sure why Mom woke up, however, I'd like to think it was from a medication I found during my intense research. This medication was one I had researched in my studies and presented to the doctors at the meeting in hopes of helping my mother return. I believe it led to a few hours of having my mother back. It did what it was known to do, if only temporarily, and we were thrilled.

Who wouldn't opt for a few hours with your loved one after not being able to experience them, in their entirety, for so long? For this time, we were given, I was, and am, grateful we tried it, and it delivered those beautiful moments.

The search for the facility was painful, as we were finding out there were no facilities nearby for patients in Mom's condition, the condition being a woman of her age, now eighty-five, having a tracheostomy and being unresponsive, and unable to participate in therapy. Ludicrous! How is one supposed to have a chance at rehabilitation if you don't exercise them or put them through the paces of therapeutic care? We received the same answers. It's as though once life throws you a curveball, and you are rendered helpless, you get no help. They just don't fight for you when you have reached that point, especially when you're elderly.

We finally found a nursing home with a respiratory care specialty floor and rehab, so we visited. I cried right there in front of the staff. I hated it. It looked old to me, and not what I had envisioned. I wanted more for Mom, although nothing would've been good enough.

Don't get me wrong, most, would find it adequate, with its cheery hallways, pretty flooring, and pleasant views. Patients appeared well cared for, but to me, I wanted more. To be honest, I wanted her home, after all I had promised. We settled her in the rehab center in late August, feeling better, knowing she'd have respiratory care and rehab, depending on her consciousness. September came and went, and we visited every day from 1 p.m. to 8 p.m., by her side all day, talking to her about our lives, playing music in her ears, grooming her, and sharing news, all in hopes of getting that miracle.

In October, during one of my daily visits, I noticed Mom didn't look well. She was flushed and noisy, and I brought it to the attention of the doctor, nurses, and respiratory caregivers. They assured me she was well. The next day, she seemed worse, and I insisted they bring her to the hospital. After much testing, the doctor called me.

He was a thoracic specialist from Boston General Hospital and came down to perform surgeries locally when needed. He informed me that Mom had a massive abscess in her lung, and it had been there for quite some time.

He stated, "It's a Coke can size, and they missed it at the hospital." Even though she was in the respiratory Intensive care unit for months, they missed it! He continued to inform me that, to remove it, they would have to deflate her lung to remove the infection, and due to her age, her lung would most likely not reinflate. I answered with, "Can't you aspirate it?" "Well, that's a possibility," he said, surprised. "Well, let's do it," I responded anxiously. So they went forward with the aspiration, and it was a huge success! What a victory! I'm no doctor, and I still shake my head when I think about how dire the situation was and how I was offered no other options. There I was, a person with no medical training, and I suggested what I felt was the least invasive option on my own, and he agreed. Why wasn't I given that option? Why didn't the specialist from Boston think of that? Why? I still can't answer that, but one thing's for sure, you are fighting for your loved one, fight like you've never fought before because you need to be the best advocate you can be. What if I didn't suggest that? Would they have given up? Was it her age? I'm pretty sure I'd say yes to those questions. Thank God I was able to come up with that option through the grace of God.

Where else did it come from? Days after surgery, Mom was settled back in the rehab center. We arrived at the center to the nurses running towards us, "Have you seen her yet?! "No, why?" I ask. "She's awake!" She even said good morning to us today"! "No!" We yelled in disbelief and pure excitement as we hurried to her room. We entered her room, and there was Mom! smiling, eyebrows lifting, and looking surprised! My Dad was floating on air, and we couldn't be happier! We greeted her with loud hellos, kisses, and lots of excitement! We spent the afternoon taking pictures and calling my brother and sister. She laughed when my sister was reliving a memory of one of their day adventures out of town and mouthed, "What happened?" When I told her she had been in a coma, she looked surprised and mouthed, "Coma?" We explained that she had been sleeping and not feeling well for a while, and now, after surgery for an infection, she was awake, and that's why we were so excited. She looked at us in bewilderment, as if we were making too much of her, like one looks when you are singing to them on their birthday or saying nice things about them. She didn't understand all the fuss, but we were giddy and eating up every minute.

Another victory! This day was heaven on earth.

The following day, we received glowing reports of Mom speaking to nurses in her usual kind way, and yes! they heard her. I'm not sure how they could have heard her voice. When you have a tracheostomy in your airway, your voice isn't audible, but somehow her voice broke through for them. Oh, how I wish we could have heard her beautiful voice, once more.

The next day, we arrived at the center, to find Mom sitting up, in a chair with the therapist kneeling in front of her. She smiled when she saw us, and the therapist remarked that we were obviously someone Mom loved, as she could tell by that smile. We watched as the therapist worked with Mom and how she responded. It appeared that her legs hurt when she exercised. 'Ow," she said and reached for her legs. She followed commands, and we were all so hopeful, so, so hopeful. It was as though my soul returned to my pained body as if new life had been given to us. This miracle was what we had prayed so hard for, and so, many, many thanks went up to God.

During this time, Matthew and his wife had a baby boy, making Julie, a Grandmother, and Mom and Dad, Great Grandparents!

Oh, how we wished Mom could have been there, as she would have been thrilled. William was named after my father and called Liam for short. He was the mirror image of Matthew. Dad cried when he saw him, wishing Mom could be there for this happy occasion. Julie brought in pictures to show Mom the new baby, and, most days, she would just stare at them. While visiting, one afternoon, I decided to show her the baby pictures again, but this time, Mom mouthed the word "cute!" We were thrilled she was able to see him in the photo and excited to tell her that we gave the new baby one of the hats she knitted. She would have adored him, and I believe she is lovingly watching over Liam. We were thankful, grateful, and elated, if just for a short time.

Mom didn't stay alert for long, maybe a day or two. She was sleeping most of the day. We were thankful and hopeful with her wake times. I would clean her mouth with the suction brush, and she could follow instructions. "Open up Mom," she would smile, and I would cheer loud enough that the nurses would comment.' It's nice that you encourage your mom. 'We can hear you in the hallways. Frankly, I didn't care who heard me or how I sounded.

Some family members would say, "She's not a baby, Jen," and "You sound like you are dealing with a child," But I didn't care. Encouragement is encouragement, and we all need it no matter what age we are, especially when we are facing challenges and health complications, so I kept cheering, clapping, and woo-hoooing, and she smiled. That, right there, made it all worth it.

By November, her alert times were less frequent, although frequent they never were. On many a visit, Mom never responded, not a flinch. We could see where this was going, but by now, we were holding on as tight as can be, trying to keep her. We couldn't bear the thought of the alternative. After sitting for eight hours at the bedside, Dad and I would ride the forty-five-minute ride home, sometimes in silence for miles, sometimes in hope, if we ever saw anything promising. The road home was the same road we had all taken, so many, many days when Mom was with us. This route was the same way home from a day of out-of-town shopping and going for lunch. My mind would wander as we rode along, passing by all the familiar places we would often stop to get donuts, gas, eat, or explore, except now her beautiful face was no longer in my rearview mirror, sitting in the back with my daughter laughing away or knitting. I still look in my rearview mirror for her face and often whisper, "Hi, Mom." What I would give, what I would give. We'd arrive back in town and update the family on her highs and lows of the day. We'd grab food from a drive-through or take out and try to breathe. We were hanging on by a thread, every single minute.

The phone was a great source of fear for me, and when it rang, my heart would jump, and our worst fears would surface. We never relaxed. I'd bring Dad home by 11:30 p.m. as he found it hard to be alone, so he stayed late. Once home, I'd settle him in and drive home by midnight. This was our routine for ten months.

I would arrive home, call the center to check on Mom, speak to the nurse, and pray to God to watch over her. I was terrified every minute. I mean, every minute. When your loved one's care is in someone else's hands, there is no worse feeling, and I hated it. I didn't sleep. I researched, prayed, and worried. I waited for that damn phone to ring, and by morning I would drift off for a few hours to wake up and do it all over again.

I'd face the day with more ideas and more hope that maybe, just maybe, this would be the day God would answer our prayers. I started each day believing and ended each day questioning.

CHAPTER 23

If Only

After ten months of being hospitalized full-time, it was now November. The trees were bare after a brilliantly colorful autumn, and it was cold. Car troubles started, and I was unable to drive my car, which also meant I couldn't make our daily visits. I priced rental cars, but the prices were outrageous, and I thought the repairs would be completed sooner rather than later. My sister agreed to come over and pick us up, and we visited three to four times a week. She filled in for some of our time in the evening. I hated it with all my heart not being able to be with her and supervising her care. Looking back, I know I should've paid for that rental car. It would have been more than worth it. Hindsight is twenty-twenty, always. Infuriating, but painfully true.

Those few days turned into two weeks before my car was repaired. Why do these things happen at the worst of times?

Mom seemed to be fading now, much less responsive, and her system was showing concerning medical issues. With random bleeding and more transfusions, I demanded a colonoscopy. They were only able to do a sigmoidoscopy because she couldn't be put under anesthesia as it was too risky, and it came back as diverticulitis. With all my heart, mind, body, and soul, I can say now I know they were wrong.

Cancer doesn't run in the family at all, and I don't know this, to be exact, but I'm here to say that I am one hundred percent sure, in my heart, that she had something they missed. Further research on my behalf also solidifies that belief. For the year previously, Mom had been saying," Is my stomach bloated?" We'd reply, "No, Mom, you have no tummy, it's flat." "I feel like it is, I really do," she would say. Do you remember when I told you about her buying the bathing suit and how hopeful we were? When she tried it on, she commented about her stomach being bloated and that she felt it. She felt something was different for some time. She had an upcoming doctor's appointment in days and a colonoscopy scheduled later that year. How I wish I were wrong. I wish I had thought of that during all of this.

I even wish they tested her for more, but the cold, hard facts are that sometimes these things can happen deep in our body unbeknownst to us and the doctors. I often think about this and what course of action we could have or would have taken. What would she have chosen?

CHAPTER 24

The End of a Journey

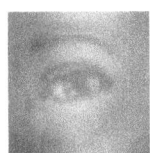

The most emotional chapter in my heart. The end of a journey, but the beginning of another. How do we say goodbye? We shouldn't, as it isn't goodbye, it's see you soon. If only letting go was this easy. If only we could all stand around the bed of our loved ones and cheer them on, wish them well on their journey ahead, and rejoice when they do. If only, however, we are weak with the emotion of what could have been or was supposed to be. It's okay to feel like we do. We don't understand loss and can make no sense of it. So we mourn what we knew, what we had. In missing our loved ones, we must learn to live without them.

We have to relearn how to live our lives. Our routines change and the things we thought were important suddenly take on new meanings. Death, as they call it, leaves the living in turmoil. It leaves us lost, depressed, and lonely. Suddenly, we are cast out into a world we don't understand.

That day began like most. Mom was in the hospital, a different hospital. Earlier in the week, the facility called to tell me that Mom was dying and that there was nothing more that they could do. I insisted that she be taken to the hospital, and they refused. They put me on speakerphone, and now the doctor was arguing with me, still refusing to send her to the hospital. I wasn't giving in and threatened to have a police escort if they didn't call the ambulance. My car was still in repair, so Julie and Ken went to the hospital. They waited as the ambulance carrying our beautiful mother arrived at the hospital Emergency room entrance.

They were bedside when Mom was brought into the emergency room, and she appeared as though she was nearing the end of her journey. The doctor examined her when he turned her and found a stage four bedsore. He groaned and gasped.

The rehab center knew she had a small abrasion, but they assured us she was being treated properly. I had asked to see it, and it appeared to be minor, just a month before. Now, it was stage four? We were devastated, as I had asked every day about that spot, every single day. I insisted that she receive an air mattress. I requested the wound care specialist, and we were told she was caring for Mom's wound. They lied!

This is why they didn't want her to go to the hospital. Mom was admitted with severe bleeding, and once again, no one could tell where it was coming from, as she was too ill to withstand the proper testing. Days after she was admitted, I was asked to come to the hospital to sign hospice consent forms. This care would make Mom more comfortable, but no heroic measures, as it could break her ribs, causing more suffering than she was already experiencing. I cried because I didn't want to give up. I wanted assurance that it meant they would still fight for her, if possible, that if it were something treatable, they would treat it. They assured me they would, and I reluctantly and painfully signed my name to release my mother from more pain.

I'll never forget the feeling in that hallway, as if she was there, watching over me, almost thanking me, but I felt I had abandoned her. I felt like I had left her to her illness, with no armor to shield her or fight for her.

We returned to her room, and the nurse arrived to tell us she was being moved upstairs to a different floor. We weren't sure why, but they said they needed the room. While they were transferring Mom to the new room, we decided to visit my brother on the surgical floor below. It just so happened he was having emergency surgery for a hernia that had strangulated. We arrived in his room soon after he came out of recovery. He was groggy as the nurse was typing into the computer. We told him Mom was being moved and wasn't doing well. He responded that he knew and someone had told him Mom was in her last hours. The nurse turned and assured him that she didn't know and that no one had told him about his mother. He insisted they had, but they had not. Was it Mom? Has she visited him in his sleep to say goodbye? We left to go to Mom, now settled into her new bed and private room. Did they know? Soon, Mom's breathing began to change. "Are you going to let her just breathe like that, with no oxygen on?" I asked. "Like what?" the nurse replied. She turned, and her face dropped. Things changed quickly. Fast-walking nurses in and out, respiratory in and out, stethoscope to her chest, they walk out saying nothing. Soon, doctors arrived to tell us that they knew that morning that the end was near. I begged them to help, tears streaming down my face. "Can't you do something?" "No, you signed up for hospice," they replied, "Well, I'll unsign it," I replied," It was just moments ago," I pleaded," pleeeease," "No, it wouldn't matter, your Mom is tired, and it's time, I'm sorry." I felt like a small child begging and pleading, crying. I felt like I'd let her down. Oh, good God. We turn towards each other with helpless hearts and looks of despair. My sister, myself, and my father are all helpless.

My Mother was nearing the end of her story, and there was nothing we could do. We held her, kissed her, sang to her, and told her all the things we wanted to say. We prayed, and then she unexpectedly opened her eyes. They were as green as Evergreen and wide-open. The nurse said she was rallying. Who was she looking for? Who was missing? I placed my cheek next to her lips, and she softly kissed my cheek. My sister replied, "My brother, my brother is missing." My Father rushed over to look into her eyes, and just then, by some miraculous intervention, my brother appeared in the room, IV poles in hand, hospital gown opened, my brother appeared. No one told him how to get there. No one guided him. He just appeared, somehow. He found the room, walked over to her, pressed his forehead onto hers, spoke quietly, and kissed her. We were all crying, and then my sister said it was time. My Father stepped in front of my brother and kissed her lips, and Mom was carried by the angels, at that very moment. He sobbed," My darlin,' my darling." I sobbed. We all cried. The nurse shut the doors as my pained cries could be heard, throughout the halls. The doctor came in and listened. It was true Mom had finished her journey.

We stayed for two hours with her, talking and crying, holding her hand, and saying our goodbyes. I kissed her one last time. We all did. I still don't know how I left that room that night. How did I walk away? How? Numbly, we passed the nurses in the dimly lit hallway. They offer their condolences as we press the elevator button down. All we had known, all we had fought for, was now just gone. A silence louder than the universe surrounded us as we stood waiting in the dark entrance for a ride. My sister's husband picked us up for a silent, lost ride home. Staring up at the stars, I remember thinking she was no longer present here with us. Dear God, what will we do? Arriving at Dad's, my sister ran in with Dad so he could grab some necessities to sleep over at my house. I waited in the car, looking at the trees outlined against the salmon-colored winter night sky.

By now, it was about 1:30 a.m. My daughter was home and had been calling, but I told her I'd be home soon, never letting on to what had happened, as she was home alone, and I didn't want her to cry alone upon hearing her best friend went to paradise. You see, their relationship was one-of-a-kind. They were pals and kindred souls, as they would say, "the same." To this day, Felicia feels she can't truly smile the same way ever again. I walked into my house with my Father, and my daughter said, "What's wrong?" "Nannies gone." I cried. She cried, and we held each other. Dad fell asleep, and I called my best friend to pass on the sad news. She comforted me and listened to my sobs. We all fell asleep from sheer exhaustion, Felicia by my side, our hearts shattered into a million pieces. The funeral was what she would have wanted. We had a Catholic mass and her favorite hymns. The only thing we didn't do, that she wanted us to do, was to have a FUN-eral. She wanted us to celebrate when she passed. She'd say," Just think how wonderful it is that I get to be with Jesus."

She loved that thought, and I'd say that gives me some joy in knowing that. One thing's for sure, I'd forget my name before I forgot you, Mom. You alone are the very reason I'm able to carry on, as you taught me there is an eternity waiting, and I can't wait to see you again. Until then, come with me, my first love, guide me, and wait for me, for you are, and always will be, loved.

Mom was a gift to my daughter, and I mean that with all my heart. They always got along famously and often would finish each other's sentences, laughing and saying "the same." Oh, how they laughed. It was uncanny, always on the same wavelength. Mom would fill her head and heart with wisdom about life and to always be true to herself. Pals, they called themselves, and I wasn't a bit jealous. I love my mother and my daughter. How could I begrudge my daughter the love and special relationship she shared with my mother? That would have been a sin, a total shame. Felicia and I are very close, with a great Mother-and-daughter relationship and best friends. I never felt threatened by my daughter's intense relationship with my mother. I wanted her to experience this unique love, this beautiful angel of a woman. It's a once-in-a-lifetime chance. With all that we gave Felicia, all the loving encouragement when Felicia was ill, all the therapy, all the tears, and laughter, Felicia learned to give it right back. She loved her Nana, and I was thrilled that she had this relationship in her life, a gift of a lifetime. Felicia would say," I love you, Mom, with all my heart. You are the best. There is no one like you Mom, except Nana. I don't love her more than I love you, I love her differently." I got it, I knew what she meant wholeheartedly, and I loved it. When Nana got sick, Felicia was right there, holding her hand, giving back the same wisdom and encouragement she had received. She would care for Nana, bathe her, dress her, and care for any needs. When Nan went to live in Heaven, Felica said she took a piece of her heart with her, but my mother prepared her, and it worked wonders.

I swear, she is a rock, much stronger than me, that's certain. All the days I sobbed and sobbed, she would get up, come over to me, hold me, kiss me, and speak incredible words of wisdom and comfort taught to her by my mother. I was so incredibly proud that my daughter, who, at one time, was so sick, was now stronger than most. She believed with all her heart what she was, taught, and lived it. She took hold of all the lessons we taught her and applied them to her life.

These beliefs are how she gets through. She knows Nana holds her in her heart, and she holds Nana in hers. She talks about her every day and shares fond memories. When I asked Felicia how she stays so strong and doesn't fall apart, she replied, "Because I know where she is, and Nana told me she would save a place for me." Her incredible kindness and wisdom shine through every day. She is a remarkable young lady. I tell her all the time she is one of the strongest people I have ever known, no doubt.

She now helps me daily with my dad, her Pop, whom she also loves dearly. Pop stepped in as a positive male image in the absence of her father, so there was nothing she wouldn't do for him. In his sickest moments, she was there to help me get him through it. Once you reach this woman's heart, you are one lucky soul. I'm so eternally grateful that Felicia got to experience the gift of my mother. I'm sure Mom is delighted with who she has become.

Dad has lost his best friend, and he could barely walk at the funeral. What was he going to do without his only love? He was now eighty-six and had been with Mom since they were sixteen. When Mom was nearing the end of her earthly journey, I promised her I'd take good care of Dad. I really believe this made her choice easier as she had spent sixty-five years with Bill and always worried about him. My brother stayed with Dad for quite a while, helping him with paperwork, etc. These days were a blur for Dad. All hope had been drained, from his soul. He cried so much that it broke my heart, and we worried this could lead to losing him, as well.

Somehow, we managed Christmas late that year, but not without so many tears. Nothing about life would ever be the same. To keep Dad from falling apart, we kept busy. Daily rides through Historic Newport, he relieved all his best memories, though sometimes the tears would stream down his face. Getting out was the best solution. If only for a moment, it occupied his mind with some normalcy. It never took away the pain or the harsh reality, as Mom was larger than life. Years later, we continue to keep him busy. My brother and sister come twice a month to take him out for lunch and spend time with him. My brother will also mow the lawn and stay late to chat or watch television together. Felicia and I spend all the other days with him. Not a day goes by when he is alone or not cared for, and we feel so happy we can be there for him, as he always has been there for us.

This quality care and time has allowed us to have him for so many more years than we could have ever imagined, and for that, we are most grateful, and I'm sure Mom would be pleased.

CHAPTER 25

Grief

Grief is the feeling of total, utter devastation. Feeling as if your heart has been ripped from your chest, trying to live without a heartbeat. Desolation, emptiness, the world swallows you whole. No one to help. No one to reach out to. No one to stop the un-relentless pain, screaming at the top of your lungs, begging God to bring them back, hoping for that one miracle. Maybe, just maybe, you could be the first person whose loved one returns because God heard you and decided to make that miracle just for you. Grief is the reality that they don't return. God doesn't reach down and pat your back. He doesn't stop the world. He just doesn't. The big question is why? Why doesn't he? Why doesn't he help us in our deepest pain? And all of my despair, I've decided on the answer, for me anyway. You'll have to come to your answer on your own. But my grief has led me to my answer. When our loved one is sick, suffering, or in an accident, we all ask why.

We look to God to intervene. It's human nature to look to our God when we are helpless. We've all learned how to pray to whatever God we believe in when it's beyond what we can control or handle. Can you imagine a world where children didn't suffer or die? Can you imagine a world where our loved ones never passed on unexpectedly or expectantly? A world without loss, a world without tears.

Life is a test. A world in which we have free will. We'll suffer at the hands of others or just fate, and in turn, we turn towards God or away from him. Based on the depth of hell you've been through, that's your choice, and not for anyone to judge how you arrived at that choice. It's how you deal with what you have. Some people live seemingly charmed lives, perfect families, great marriages, and hardly a bad day, whereas some suffer greatly. They say, do good work, and good will come back to you. Give, and you will get. Care for your parents in their weakest days, and you will be rewarded. Is it true? Well, I beg to differ. Mom did all those wonderful things and still suffered in the end. Children are innocent, yet they suffer. Jesus himself suffered, so what's it all about? What's my answer? My answer is most likely not much different from yours. I don't know how it all works, but I do know that God intervenes in ways we don't control.

If you believe in life after death and Jesus, then he intervenes by taking our loved ones to peace, to a place where suffering doesn't exist, to a place where there is only happiness and love. Now that is a gift. That is the answer to a prayer that surpasses all.

I like to think that in our darkest hours of suffering, we are blessed with a choice. If shown a world, where hurt doesn't exist, what would you choose? A world where unconditional love and peace surround us. How can we blame anyone for choosing that? How grateful should we be that that place exists? Jesus suffered and died so that we will have eternity with our loved ones, never to hurt or be apart again, and for this, I'm thankful and most grateful. Stop looking for the answers. Stop looking for justice. Just have faith that in our last moments, we will be given the choice or the choice will be made for us. Don't allow Jesus's death to be in vain. Be kind, be gentle, and be patient. Give your weaknesses to God, and stop searching here for the answers. The answers aren't here. They are all waiting. So, in the meantime, be ready to answer the question, What did you do with the life I gave you?

Turn grief into a proclamation of love and a legacy. Tell their story. Laugh and smile at the good memories you had, and hold in your heart. Rejoice in their newly found peace, in their new home, where there is no pain, only joy, all burdens forgotten. They have arrived. They have been released from this world of free will, injustice, and earthly existence. They passed the test, and if they are loved so intensely, that your grief is beyond measure, you can be sure there is a place in God's house for them. Surely, they were not perfect, as none of us are. In God's house, they will learn, repent, and earn their place.

So, you see, my grief isn't any less now than it was. My grief has found a place to allow me to breathe and rejoice in my loved ones' joy. It's selfless love. I am happy for my Mom.

I am filled with peace that she is with Jesus, rejoicing in a place of pureness and beauty. That is the true definition of love. It's loving them so much that you let them go so they can experience Jesus and his glory. In my mother's last earthly moments, I prayed, "Lord, if you can't save her, then take her." He did just that. My beautiful Mother joined Jesus, was released from her broken, beautiful shell, and gently taken to heaven.

When Mom's sister passed, she found peace in knowing that she was pain-free and released into the arms of Jesus. This faith allowed her to rejoice for her sister with selfless love. She missed her big sister terribly and would often talk about her. She missed her visits and their phone calls but was so thankful to sing to her one last time over the phone. It broke Mom's heart as she loved her sister dearly and truly enjoyed being with her. When Mom finished singing to her sister, Irma spoke, "That was beautiful, Victoria, just beautiful." Irma had been unresponsive and nearing the end of her journey, and after hearing her sister Victoria's voice, she spoke. Love is strong, and Mom was in tears.

She was happy she had the chance to comfort her big sister and always rejoiced that she was set free despite missing her so badly. Selfless love. When her father passed away, they performed chest compressions. Mom was pained by their actions as she didn't want him to suffer. Again, selfless love. I believe that our soul is who we are and that our bodies are just vessels housing our soul while we walk the earth in this lesson of life. The soul is energy, and energy never ceases. I choose to believe that my mother is still very much alive in spirit, in fact, more so than you and me.

She can experience all the beauty all the time and is still very much a part of our lives. Heaven, or paradise, in my opinion, is another chapter we reach when our life's purpose has been achieved. We continue to learn and love and await a reunion of our loved ones. So, in turn, I still talk to Mom. I will include her in my days as I would if she were still physically here. Sometimes, I feel her as though she is still physically here. Who am I to question this? I don't know if it's possible. We don't have the answers. I know as a mother, I would want to be nearby. I choose to feel my mother, to make our love go beyond the distance between us, if any, and still believe we are together, as we've always been my… entire… life.

CHAPTER 26

Love Transcends

What is love? A bond between people, connected by the heart. The feeling of safety, comfort, and warmth all wrapped up in that special someone. Love is knowing that nothing can tear you apart, not time or distance. Love is everlasting. Love can't be taken, or tarnished, only cherished,... love. Can we love someone who isn't here? Yes, and even deeper than you loved them when they were present in the physical form. Love is experienced in spirit and the deepest of our hearts. Love is sacred above all others, untouched, magical, and without barriers. There's something amazingly- special when you love someone who is now living in the presence of Jesus. In your heart, you know all their burdens have been forgotten, all questions answered, and peace finds a place in your soul, with a connection that transcends all distances we

194

think to exist. You may have heard of the invisible
cord. That cord is made intricately out of love. I assure
you; that eternal love is the most beautiful love you
will ever experience. It will carry you through your
darkest days, and you will feel it if you let it. Close
your eyes. Can you see them? Touch their hands. Do
you feel them? This love is the most unique, special
love you will ever feel, and it's yours only. Can you
imagine? It will never end, lasting for all eternity. Now,
only now, have you loved them in their entirety, for
love knows no barriers, no distance. Love is forever.
Hold tight, breathe deeply, close your eyes, SHHH...I'm
right here. I'm right here...

CHAPTER 27

The Aftermath

Survival is the state of one's mind after trauma, the ruins. That is the aftermath. Losing a loved one is always a tremendous loss. Losing a loved one traumatically is a loss of them and you. To watch a loved one suffer, fight, and go through medical procedures you never thought you'd see is the most helpless feeling in the world. Love is powerful, for when we love deeply, we think nothing of trading places with our loved ones. I would've jumped right in that bed if it meant she was well again, but we don't get to make that choice. So, we sit nervously beside them, praying and doing everything we can to change their outcome, for the better. When it comes to an end, we are defeated, broken, and traumatized. Some folks come out of trauma with a mission, some force happiness into their lives, now knowing how fragile and short life is, and some of us die, never to be found again. Those of us, who have been on this terrible journey of helplessness, and grief, are never the same. We can't be.

When life veers off the unthinkable road, we are all damaged. We leave who we were on the high road, and now we find ourselves trying to crawl back up that cliffside, not knowing if we even want to reach the top. After all, the high road can lead to pain and a lot of it. So, I chose the middle road. I'll crawl back up, but not where I had been before because I can't. I no longer exist. Jennifer no longer exists. Jennifer died on the high road, and life threw me right off the cliff. So, the middle road feels better. It's a new place to start, a new place to build the new me. It's a safer place to tread lightly. I don't trust the way things were before. I used to think my **faith** was almost like an "insurance policy" that would protect me if I believed. I found that my "Insurance policy," had a clause, "Expect the unexpected."

Life's tragedies can happen even when insured. So, while I'll keep my faith, I will learn to live in the moment. It's all we have. The present, the gift. I'll feel the pain of losing my Mother, physically, every day, but I will also feel joy. I will feel the immense blessing of fifty-two years of unconditional love. She was there with me and for me, as I was for her. That is joy and a lot of it. That joy is so hard to find now, in the same form it always had been. Solidly formed and beautifully designed, we stood together for so long. I long for her touch and scent, her voice, her presence. It's a world that is foreign to me, and I cry often. I used to cry so hard I thought my head would implode. I never knew pain like that existed until then, and still now. It tears you apart, pulls your insides out, and you are lost. Unfathomable despair. That is the aftermath that leads you to the middle road. Here, I hope to grow into a new version of myself. I'll take all the tools she gave me and stand tall. I will stand to make her proud. I want everyone to know who she was and all that she gave. She believed in God, had faith, loved fiercely, and prayed deeply. It has been mentioned that angels walk among us.

I know that to be true as I walked hand-in-hand with her for those fifty-two years and continue to do so through our connected souls. So middle road, I'm here with the same policy, knowing damn well I'm different. I'm still here, for now, living in the aftermath.

CHAPTER 28

Sweet Reminders

Long conversations, on the phone, dinners, and celebrations, at my home. Shopping for treasures and eating lunch are those memories I keep and miss a bunch. Chocolate chip cookies and how they smelled, grilled cheese and patty melt, made so well, the sound of your laughter filling the air, your baby's soft face and skin so fair. Your sweet scent is like fields of flowers, how I wish I could hold you for hours and hours. Beautiful gifts wrapped up like a dream, cakes made with love, sweet buttercream. Positive emotions like rivers flow, bringing joy to all wherever you go. Singsong voice as you answer hello, excited responses with a happy, loud Oh! Sweet mother of mine, I miss you, my dear, but with eyes closed, I feel you near. Licking the beaters, cookie dough, and the blimp waving at your sheet sign below. The waves crashing over the car one day, don't tell daddy let's get away. Adventurous fun, full of love, I feel you sweet mama watch from above.

The Room

The room seems to sway as you rock back and forth. The moon peeking through my window. Your warm, soft hands caress my hair, sweeping my forehead. Shhh, Mommy's here. Sweetest of days and memories of you, beautiful voice filling the room. Enveloped safely, all fears are far, no sweeter time etched in my mind, Mother of mine. My gift.,my true love, stay with me please, stay with me, please. Show me the stars and the moon's all aglow. Never let go, please, Mom, please don't go. Lay down beside me, hold me near. Stay with me, stay, sweet memories so dear.

Lost

How does someone say goodbye to someone they've loved deeply, fiercely, and uniquely? Arms outstretched. I can't reach you, your lips on my cheek. Heaven and hell wrapped in one, love and pain all at once. Tragically, you slip away just like that. Are you okay? Wait! Wait! No, not yet. I'm not ready. Wait, my love, just one more. Guttural sobs pierce my soul.

Silently, you leave, and I die, I die. Sterile walls, dark sky, empty hearts, we sit defeated, deserted in pieces. Two hours with you, wake me up, save me, come back. Hell for me, heaven for you. Walking away, kisses and tears, shells of ourselves. Starlight sky, sorrow fills my soul. Where are you? Empty world, crushing pain. Lost without you… lost.

❋ Go With the Flow ❋

A loving Mother once firmly planted a little girl to ready her for life. She said, little one, hang on tight. Life won't be easy. The winds will howl and blow hard. They will try to uproot you, but hold on darling, stay firmly planted until the storm subsides. Then, little one, rejoice, feel the light breezes, and smell the sweet fragrance, and then, smiling, with joy in your heart, Go with the flow. (JW)

The Things I Miss About You

I miss you, the smell of your softness when I hugged you, the floral scent I breathed in. Your laughter when I asked what perfume you had on, and you'd reply, "Sorry, no perfume, it's just me." Yes, just wonderful you. I miss your voice. Everything about your voice made me smile. Your enthusiasm and song, talking for hours, laughing, and crying.

Advice and life stories. The sad, the bad, the good, our calls held it all. One day, soon after you left, your phone rang once, and the number came through as your number. The message was simple, softly spoken, "Hi," Was it you, Mom? On my birthday, the phone rang at our usual time three times in a row. Someone was there but did not speak. Was it you?

I miss you every second of every day, yet I know you remain. I'll carry you and bring you with me. I'll cry and laugh and still shake my head. I look up and look around. I'm aware that you surround me everywhere. I am eternally grateful, incredibly blessed, and still loving you. There is no end. I know the best is yet to come. Wait, sweet mother, I must finish the journey you sent me on, and when I do, I will run to you with open arms, smell your sweet scent once again, rejoice in our love, and never... Let...You...Go

CHAPTER 29

Happy Birthday

Happy Birthday to you, Happy birthday to you, Happy birthday, Dear Jennifer, Happy birthday to you! Speech! Speech! That little song with her powerful, beautiful, operatic voice I miss so much, year after year. Mom would sing loudly and beautifully, often harmonizing at the end, clap and yell, speech, speech! Oh, how I miss that. On the day of our birthday, Mom always made sure to call and sing over the phone, and if you weren't home, she'd sing on the answering machine. I saved over fifty voice recordings but somehow failed to capture that one. I kick myself every birthday that I don't hear her voice. Birthdays are the day we are born, forever celebrated. Life is so precious. We all gather year-to-year for each other's birthdays and rejoice. We made it another year. No matter how difficult the year has been, we celebrate. If life has been difficult, we often celebrate larger, louder, and harder. We made it through. Good or bad, we're still here, so we blow out the candles.

It is the story of our lives, every single one of our lives, one day at a time until that day rolls around again if we're lucky. We made it through. Good or bad, we're still here, so we blow out the candles. It is the story of our lives, every single one of our lives, one day at a time until that day rolls around again if we're lucky. When you die, do your birthdays stop? I suppose, in reality, they do. Can we celebrate another year? I have chosen to keep celebrating Mom's birthday every year. I get a cake and candles and put her earthly age on top. Why? I'm celebrating the day my beautiful Mother was born, the day Jesus sent an angel, a wonderful little girl who grew up to be a wonderful Mother who made a difference in our lives and many others. I never want to forget that day. I intend to celebrate Mom's birthday every year. In my opinion, it is a monumental day. The day God gave me my Mother. What a gift! She celebrated eighty-four birthdays and one while sleeping, and I will continue to celebrate your wonderful day until my last day. I'll cheer, and I'll yell, speech, speech! Have a cake, and make a wish. A wish that I'm positive will come true. Happy birthday, Mom. I'll celebrate you, always.

Chapter 30

She Is

By now, I'm sure you have a picture of who my Mom is. Perhaps I was redundant in telling you so. No matter how many words I have written or how big a book I write, I could never fill it with enough words about my Mother. What more can I say? My Mother was a blessing from God. She is ours, and more importantly, she is God's. We are blessed and forever changed because of her. Mom had always stressed to her children that there was only one thing that was important for her children to know. Mom wanted us to know how much she loved us. Mom extended comfort to us, even in her darkest days. I would sit beside her in the Intensive Care Unit, hold her hand, and rest my head on the side rails. One day, Mom reached up and started to rub my hair. She always did that, all my life, even when she was fighting for hers. I will always carry that beautiful memory in my heart.

Mom was so sick, yet she was still wanting to comfort me. My brother snapped a picture that I will treasure forever. Only a mother's love. I was so blessed. Can you imagine how fortunate we are? So, when the wind blows too hard and the darkest storms hover, when all else fails, and we are about to crumble, we know we are loved. In life, there can be no sweeter gift. Mom often wondered if she was worthy of the Lord. I whispered she was. I hope you are sitting at the feet of Jesus, Mom. I hope your sweet voice fills the heavens as you walk along, hand in hand with Jesus. I hope you are laughing with your family, whom you missed so dearly, and I hope you know we loved you with every fiber of our souls, and, Yes Mom, oh yes, we know you loved us beyond measure. You showed it, we felt it, we cherished it. We adored you from day one, under your heart, until today inside your heart. We are in awe of you, Mom, and your unique love. We know no amount of distance can separate us, and your spirit is alive and at peace.

You are in my heartbeat, and I feel your touch when I close my eyes. You're right here. I can feel you, smell you, and you encompass me. Stay with me, come along, guide me, celebrate with me, comfort me, feel my love, and know that if I lived a thousand lifetimes, I'd never find, *A Love Like This... Lovingly forever, your baby, Jennifer*

IN LOVING MEMORY OF MY WONDERFUL MOTHER

ACKNOWLEDGMENTS

First and foremost, I want to thank my wonderful Mother, Victoria. Without her love, this book would not be possible. This is your story, Mom. I love you so very much my sweet angel. Thank you for everything, you are a gift, and I feel you every day. My love for you is eternal. I am blessed to have your immense love. My best friend, my soulmate, I adore you.

Thank you to my dear daughter, who had incredible patience while I spent so much of my time writing. Thank you, Felicia, for rooting me on, and telling me all the right things, for helping me when my mind went blank or when the tears were streaming down my face, reading this to you. I just love your positivity. Thank you for being so supportive, encouraging me, and giving me the strength, and wisdom I needed. Thank you for making all of us laugh, especially Nana, and for being her kindred spirit. I love you more than life. You are amazing!

To my Father, thank you for all the memories, for being such an intricate part of Mom's story, and for being the best Dad and Grandfather. I love you so much, and I'm so grateful for your love and dedication to us.

To my brother Ken, and sister Julie, Weren't we lucky?

To my lifelong friend, Tammy. Thank you for being there, the countless phone calls, listening to me cry my heart out for hours, for years, no matter what time it was and for how long, you listened. Thank you for the right words when I thought I couldn't bear the pain. Thank you for not giving me a timeline on my grief, and letting me know you cared.

END

www.ingramcontent.com/pod-product-compliance
Lightning Source LLC
Chambersburg PA
CBHW060508130626
46553CB00002B/434

* 9 7 9 8 9 8 9 1 9 2 3 0 4 *